"Steve hits the heart issues. Following Jesus is not about behavior—it's about heart. Steve's book helps you know who you are, and who you are drives how you behave."

—Dr. Barry St. Clair
president & founder, Reach Out Youth Solutions

"*How to Stay Christian in High School* has captured the core issues necessary for any teen to walk tall on today's campuses. I highly recommend this resource."

—Dr. Dann Spader
executive director, Sonlife Ministries

"Steve Gerali has done a wonderful job of taking teenagers from the Bible and retelling their stories in a relevant and captivating way without losing the biblical truth. High school students will easily identify with the issues that these teenagers were facing and learn from their stories."

—K.J. Stephens
youth pastor, Orange County, California

"Steve did it again. This real look into the lives of biblical teens as they might have sounded and lived today delivers an incredible message of love, truth, purity, and freedom. What a great book for students to think through and plug into their lives."

—Joshua Ott
youth pastor, Grace Evangelical Free Church, Cressona, Pennsylvania

"There is nothing more appealing to the church than to see students on fire and passionately living for God! Steve hits the nail on the head in helping a student understand whose we are. A must read for every teenager."

—Tim Block
senior pastor, Canyon Ridge Bible Church, Chandler, Arizona

"Steve Gerali did a superb job of smoothly connecting story, Scripture, and getting into the lives of teens today. How refreshing to see young Bible characters being placed into our twenty-first century to bring hope to Christian kids in high school today."

—Michael L. Beatty
commissioned minister, mokualkaua Cong'l Church Kailua-Kona, Hawaii.
program director for Christian Endeavor Hawaii

Go Ahead :

TH1NK: *about God*

about life

about others

Faith isn't just an act; it's something you live—something huge and sometimes unimaginable. By getting into the real issues in your life, TH1NK books open opportunities to talk honestly about your faith, your relationship with God and others, as well as all the things life throws at you.

Don't let other people th1nk for you . . .

TH1NK for yourself.

HOW
TO STAY
CHRISTIAN
IN HIGH SCHOOL

Steve Gerali

TH1NK Books
an imprint of NavPress®

TH1NK is an imprint of NavPress.

TH1NK and the TH1NK logo are registered trademarks of NavPress. Absence of ® in connection with marks of NavPress or other parties does not indicate an absence of registration of those marks.

ISBN 1-57683-424-7

Cover design by BURNKIT
Creative Team: Jay Howver, Gary Wilde, Arvid Wallen, Darla Hightower, Glynese Northam

Unless otherwise identified, all Scripture quotations in this publication are taken from the HOLY BIBLE: NEW INTERNATIONAL VERSION® (NIV®). Copyright © 1973, 1978, 1984 by International Bible Society. Used by permission of Zondervan Publishing House. All rights reserved. Other versions used include: the *New American Standard Bible* (NASB), © The Lockman Foundation 1960, 1962, 1963, 1968, 1971, 1972, 1973, 1975, 1977, 1995; and *THE MESSAGE* (MSG). Copyright © 1993, 1994, 1995, 1996, 2000, 2001, 2002. Used by permission of NavPress Publishing Group.

Gerali, Steve.
  How to stay Christian in high school / Steve Gerali.
    p. cm.
  Includes bibliographical references and index.
  ISBN 1-57683-424-7
  1. High school students--Religious life. 2. Christian teenagers--Religious life. I. Title.

BV4531.3.G47 2004
248.8'3--dc22
                              2004006298

Printed in Canada

1 2 3 4 5 6 7 8 9 10 / 08 07 06 05 04

FOR A FREE CATALOG OF
NAVPRESS BOOKS & BIBLE STUDIES,
CALL 1-800-366-7788 (USA)
OR 1-416-499-4615 (CANADA)

CONTENTS

IS IT POSSIBLE TO BE CHRISTIAN IN HIGH SCHOOL?

"It's really hard to be a Christian; I *hate* it!"

That was Mark talking, right after youth group. He was a typical high school sophomore—tall, handsome, healthy, energetic, possessing a great sense of humor. Being outgoing and friendly, Mark hung out with lots of friends at school and church, and he loved to laugh and joke around. Mark also worked hard to get good grades, played soccer on the JV team at school, and had started a lawn-mowing business so he could save money for a car (when he got his license). Mark loved life. His enthusiasm was contagious.

Mark grew up in a "Christian home" from day one. The weekend after his folks brought him home from the hospital, they were in church. His family had always been active in their congregation, so Mark and his sisters never knew life apart from Christian worship and fellowship. And Mark's parents were super-busy in the congregation. In fact, they did everything from teaching Sunday school to helping on cleanup days. So Mark grew up with a love for service too. He often helped wherever he could and was a vital part of the youth group's leadership core.

Mark heard all the Bible stories in Sunday school, and he loved them. He was dedicated to the Lord as an infant, asked Jesus into his life when he was seven years old, was baptized when he was ten. He recommitted his life to Christ at junior high camp in seventh grade . . . re-recommitted his life in eighth grade . . . and re-re-recommitted his life during his freshman year of high school.

"It was so much easier being a Christian when I was little," Mark continued, as we sat down together at a table holding several bowls of leftover snacks from the meeting. "I'm really confused, because so many things about it seem contradictory. And that makes it too hard. This isn't my idea of abundant life."

"What do you mean, Mark?" I replied.

"Well, for example, I've been told all my life that Christians are supposed to be *in* the world but not *of* the world, right?"

"Right. Jesus talks about that in the gospel of John."

"Okay, so I hear my parents and my youth pastor always saying I shouldn't hang out with nonChristian friends. Christians aren't supposed to go to parties or have . . . (he makes air quotes here) . . . *'unequally yoked relationships.'* A lot of my friends at church are homeschooled or going to Christian schools. That way they can stay separated from the influences of the world. But I'm in public school, so I get attitude from my Christian friends when I miss youth group activities because of soccer. My youth pastor has even confronted me about my priorities.

"But here's the thing: Every time we have an outreach event at youth group, they tell us to bring our nonChristian friends! Can you believe that? I'm expected to be a witness to my nonChristian friends. Don't you see the mixed message—*I'm not supposed to have any nonChristian friends!* How can I have nonChristian friends if I can't hang out with them? If I can't hang out with them, then they'll only be casual friends. And you can't talk about deep things—like a relationship with Christ—with casual friends.

"I mean, I can't go up to the guys on my soccer team and just start telling them about Jesus. They don't know me, and I don't know them well enough to talk about deep stuff. So how do I beat the guilty feelings I have over not being able to 'witness' (more air quotes) when I'm not close enough to them to talk about Christ?"

I could see that Mark felt defeated. He reached out, took a couple of pretzels, and began toying with them on the table as he kept thinking. "That's not all," he continued, with a new burst of energy. "I know we can't be perfect, but we're *expected* to be perfect. Christians are supposed to be all righteous and have everything together. But then we're told we *don't* have to have it all together. But the truth is, were expected to have it all together. So how can I be expected to do something that I can't do?

"This is just another mixed message! How am I supposed to be a Christian in high school?"

TESTING THOSE MIXED MESSAGES

Can you relate to Mark? I sure can. He's committed and passionate about living for Christ. He really loves Jesus. On the other hand, I understood his frustration. He was working hard at being a Christian and being a normal teenager in high school. It seemed those two aspects of his life were always colliding, resulting in a sense of defeat.

You see, Mark is a thinker. As he thought things through, he ran headlong into contradictory messages from parents and church leaders. Yet, as he once told me, he felt guilty questioning the things he'd been taught as a kid about being a Christian.

What could I say to Mark? For one thing, I suggested that the same book of the Bible that tells him to be separated from the world also gives him permission to question and challenge the things he'd learned. For example, in 1 John 4:1, the apostle John says, "Beloved, do not believe every spirit, but test the spirits to see whether they are from God; because many false prophets have gone out into the world" (NASB).

That's right. God gives you permission to test the teachings you hear. He will faithfully reveal what's true. God won't get angry, nor will He get His feelings hurt, when you think through, question with a proper attitude, or challenge the things you hear and learn. The Holy Spirit is renewing your mind constantly. That means He is solidifying and internalizing His truth in you. He wants you to think.

That's why this is a Th1nk Book. It's *not* a big "To Do" list. It won't be filled with steps or formulas to follow for better Christian living. You see, anyone can follow a list, or mimic a pattern of behaviors, and think they are Christian. Let me explain what I mean by talking about my background for a moment. . . .

My family heritage is Italian, and I am full-blooded, 100 percent Italian. My grandparents on my father and mother's side came to the United States directly from Italy. So imagine how I felt when a friend gave me a book titled *How to Be Italian.* It listed all the funny stereotypical behaviors that Italians supposedly do, like using their hands when they talk, or saying certain phrases like "Whatsa you problem?" or "Forgetta bout it." You get the picture. "The book reminds me of you," my friend said.

As I think about that silly little book, I now realize it should be titled, *How to Act Like an Italian.* Do you see the difference? A guy like Mark could pick up the book and mimic all those so-called "Italian ways." But that wouldn't make him Italian any more than acting like a monkey would turn him into a hairy, tree-climbing chimpanzee! The point is, many people refer to actions when describing a Christian. But acting like a Christian doesn't make you one—nor does it make you a better one.

People may think that what they do defines who they are. The truth is that *who* you are defines *what* you do.

HOW THIS BOOK CAN HELP

Doing "Christian things" won't make you more of a Christian. But being a Christian will make you behave differently. So in this book we will look at what it means to *be* Christian, *think* Christian, and *behave* Christian in high school. The method is simple: Starting in chapter 2, we'll look at real teenagers in the Bible: Mary, Daniel, Joseph, brothers James and John, and Timothy. I think these teens understood that being God's person shaped how they acted. They faced the same types of pressures and problems you face today. They are not super-spiritual teen wonders. They have no great powers and no more of a "special connection" to God than you have. They are just like you. They learned how to *be* God's person, and that shaped what they *did* as people of God.

To help you see them as real, and see how they relate to you, I've retold their stories with a modern-day twist. I've imagined how some of their conversations would have flowed, based on lots of talks I've had with teens today. But the thing is, are you ready to use your imagination too? I'm inviting you to come along on this trek with an open mind, ready to think things through. I also invite you to have an open heart before God as you read. I'm going to ask you to use your imagination and step into these biblical teens' lives, conversations, and struggles. You'll probably see that they had a hard time living out their faith, just like you do.

And I'm inviting you to . . . *think.* I hope you will think long and hard about how all of this applies to you, personally, on a daily basis. As you walk through your high school, every day, remember that God is at work in you. He is making you great, through all your ups and downs, all your successes and failures. He is totally in love with you and has a plan for you that includes purpose and fulfillment.

So let's look closely at who you are in God. Ask Him to help you see how being a Christian defines your identity, shapes the way you think, and affects your behaviors.

Ask God to help you think it through.

— STEVE GERALI

"I AM" IN CHRIST

"It sounds like this is all about you and not about God, Drew."

"What do you mean?"

"Well, you're concentrating so hard on doing the right things that your attention is out of focus."

"You mean I shouldn't do anything about my temptations?" Drew asked.

"No, all I'm saying is: Focus on Him, not on the problems."

I have two teenage daughters. Almost every day, as they were growing up, I would tell them certain things that I never wanted them to forget. When they went to bed at night, when they left to go to school each day, when they went away for the weekend, I would always say: "Remember *whose* you are."

One day a friend overheard me. He said, "Don't you mean remember *who* you are?"

"No," I replied. "I know that they will have to learn about who they are. But I want them to know *whose* they are — that they belong to God and to me."

When a person trusts Christ for salvation, the Bible says many things happen to that person besides receiving eternal life. One of those things is becoming part of God's family. If you thought that all people who are created are all God's *children*, you were wrong. They are all God's *creation*, but not necessarily His children. Think about it. John 1:12-13 says, "to all who received him, to those who believed in his name, he gave the right to become children of God—children born not of natural descent, nor of human decision or a husband's will, but born of God." Paul kind of says the same thing in Galatians 3:26, stating that we are "sons of God through faith in Christ Jesus."

Only the person who trusts in Jesus is a child of God. The apostle Paul refers to it as being *in Christ*. Being God's child brings great responsibilities but it also provides great privileges. Most of the time we hear only about the responsibilities, and these often come with a list of things we have to do because we wear Christ's name. Now don't get this wrong; those responsibilities are important, and we'll talk about them later in this chapter. But if we hear only about the responsibilities, we can become discouraged.

There are privileges too. When I told my daughters to remember whose they were, I wasn't just reminding them to watch their behavior. I was also encouraging them to enjoy their family life.

So now that you're clear about whose you are, are you ready to get more specific about your own privileges and responsibilities? Let's jump in by looking at three implications of being *in Christ*. The first two focus on the privileges, and the third one focuses on the responsibility. I've come up with three words to help you remember: Ownership, Sonship, and Partnership.

WHOSE I AM IMPLIES OWNERSHIP

How well I remember the day when each of my daughters was born! Those two days are riveted into my memory forever. Years later, I recall thinking, *These two precious, wonderful, beautiful girls . . . belong to me!*

The more I thought about it, the more profound the idea became. I started to think that someday they would get married and change their names. But that didn't make them any less mine. They have my DNA. My genetic code is written through them, and no matter what, they would always belong to me. They could do nothing to change that.

That's exactly what it's like when you belong to God. Ownership means you belong to Him forever. Stop and think about that for a minute. If you are a Christian you belong to the God of the universe, the God who just speaks and things suddenly exist, who holds all things in the palm of His hand. He's the almighty, all-knowing, all-being God. He *owns* you. How cool is that?

Here's how it works. At one point, sin owned you, because you were born in sin. The book of Romans tells us that because of Adam and Eve's sin, a sinful nature was passed on from generation to generation. Carefully study the verses below to see how this generational problem unfolded . . . and then was solved through Christ.

> *You know the story of how Adam landed us in the dilemma we're in—first sin, then death, and no one exempt from either sin or death. That sin disturbed relations with God in everything and everyone, but the extent of the disturbance was not clear until God spelled it out in detail to Moses. So death, this huge abyss separating us from God, dominated the landscape from Adam to Moses. Even those who didn't sin precisely as Adam did by disobeying a specific command of God still had to experience this termination of life, this separation from God. But Adam, who got us into this, also points ahead to the One who will get us out of it.*

Yet the rescuing gift is not exactly parallel to the death-dealing sin. If one man's sin put crowds of people at the dead-end abyss of separation from God, just think what God's gift poured through one man, Jesus Christ, will do! There's no comparison between that death-dealing sin and this generous, life-giving gift. The verdict on that one sin was the death sentence; the verdict on the many sins that followed was this wonderful life sentence. If death got the upper hand through one man's wrongdoing, can you imagine the breathtaking recovery life makes, sovereign life, in those who grasp with both hands this wildly extravagant life-gift, this grand setting-everything-right, that the one man Jesus Christ provides?

Here it is in a nutshell: Just as one person did it wrong and got us in all this trouble with sin and death, another person did it right and got us out of it. But more than just getting us out of trouble, he got us into life! One man said no to God and put many people in the wrong; one man said yes to God and put many in the right. (Romans 5:12-19, MSG)

As you can see, along with the sin nature came death, making you dead . . . in sin. That means you were *in sin* — dead (owned by sin). The only solution to becoming alive is to be *in Christ.* Christ has to become your owner.

So He bought you: "You are not your own; you were bought at a price. Therefore honor God with your body" (1 Corinthians 6:19-20). What a great price was paid to buy you—the blood of Christ! Consequently, this means you are incredibly valued by God. He thinks that you are so valuable that He bought you by dying for you. Ownership means you are highly treasured—esteemed, cherished, beloved—by God.

So many times I run into Christian high school students who think they are worthless. Satan wants you to believe that lie. You are not worthless; Jesus Christ bought you, and He paid the highest price He could to own you. You may not be *worthy* of that price, but you certainly are far from *worthless*.

Being bought and owned by Christ is what theologians call the act of *redemption*. Redemption doesn't just mean you were purchased. It also implies that you were bought and then remade, new and improved. When you are in Christ, you are continuously made into a brand-new person. The old things, the old attitudes, habits, and behaviors of your sinful nature, keep on passing away or dying out. That new person God is making you into keeps on becoming new, stronger, more dominant. As Paul put it: "If anyone is in Christ, he is a new creation; the old has gone, the new has come!" (2 Corinthians 5:17). And the new keeps coming! I know this is a hard concept to grasp, but think of it like this. There is never an old; when God redeems, He only keeps making you new. You are not the same person you were a second ago because that person was changed into a new person.

God also reminds you that *He* is the one doing all the work, not you. Because *He* owns you, *He* does the work of perfecting you and maturing you. All of this reminds me of a conversation I once had with a guy named Drew.

Drew was a typical high school student who believed that God had saved him, but that he (Drew) had to work hard to prove that he was saved. Every time he messed up, he would get discouraged. One day I confronted Drew about his thinking patterns.

"You know, it sounds like this is all about *you* and not about *God*, Drew."

"What do you mean?"

"Well, it sounds as if you're concentrating so hard on doing the *right* things that your attention is not on the God who really is in control of your life. You are trusting in your own power to overcome some problem instead of trusting in the Lord to make you new. You're focusing more on the problems and on changing rather than on the God who can control the problems and is already changing you."

"Does that mean that I just shouldn't do anything about my temptations?" Drew asked.

"No, it means remembering that God started a great work in you and that He will complete that great work like Philippians 1:6 says. *He* started the work and *He* completes it. All I'm saying is: *Focus on Him, not on the problems.*"

God owns you and values you. And because He owns you, He is making you new all the time. What a relief, right?

WHOSE I AM IMPLIES SONSHIP

One day an important man came to Jesus. He didn't want anyone to see him because he was a religious leader and teacher. He was expected to have all the answers about the spiritual life. So he came at night, when there were no crowds around Jesus, to find out: *Is there a guaranteed way that I can be a part of the kingdom of God?*

Jesus answered Nicodemus's question by telling him that he needed to be born again. Well, you can imagine a grown man's reaction to that! Nicodemus had never heard such a thing before. He never read about rebirthing in any of the sacred writings. None of the prophets ever mentioned it, and Moses never wrote about it in the Law. What did Jesus mean?

Nicodemus truly wanted to be part of the *kingdom* of God; he didn't get it when Jesus started to talk about being a part of the *family* of God. But Jesus was telling Nicodemus that, as a family member, you're already in the kingdom. He explained to Nicodemus that he needed to be born spiritually into God's family. (You can read this entire story in John 3.)

Jesus talked about something the religious group had never heard. He was introducing them, and us, to the fact that we get the distinct privilege of becoming God's children. That's sonship. That carries a lot of weight.

The apostles John and Paul help us understand this more clearly. They knew what it was to be a part of God's family. John says that because we are called the sons of God this shows that God is pouring His great love on us (see 1 John 3:1). It's a love that can never separate us from God, according to Paul:

> *Who shall separate us from the love of Christ? Shall trouble or hardship or persecution or famine or nakedness or danger or sword? As it is written:*
>
> *"For your sake we face death all day long; we are considered as sheep to be slaughtered."*
>
> *No, in all these things we are more than conquerors through him who loved us. For I am convinced that neither death nor life, neither angels nor demons, neither the present nor the future, nor any powers, neither height nor depth, nor anything else in all creation, will be able to separate us from the love of God that is in Christ Jesus our Lord. (Romans 8:35-39)*

Think about it! Because you have sonship in God's family, He loves you with a great love from which you can never be separated. That love is so enormous that you can't even wrap your mind around it. It is limitless; it never has any conditions; it can never be changed, affected, or taken away. This means nothing you can do will ever even dent or put a ripple in God's love for you. Fill in the blanks:

But what if I did _____?

But what if I said _____?

But what if I thought _____?

But what if I went _____?

But what if I tried _____?

But what if I _____?

No matter what you put in those blanks . . . God would still love you.

On the other hand, Satan wants you to think that you can screw things up when it comes to God's love for you. He wants you to believe that God will love you less if you mess up. That's not true. In the Romans 8 passage that you just read, Paul supplies a list of categories that includes just about everything bad that you can think of (plus, he adds anything that you *can't* think of that would be created), and he says that because of your *sonship*, none of these things can separate you from God's love. He will never *not* love you; you're His kid. That also means He will never love someone else more than He loves you.

The other side of Satan's lie is that, while God will love you, He will love others more than you. While my wife was pregnant with our second baby, I remember worrying that I might not love this new child as much as I love my first child. I loved my first daughter so much that

I didn't think I had the capacity to love another child to the same degree. We have this idea that there is only so much love in us, and that when it's used up, well . . . it's used up. How ridiculous! I learned fast that my capacity to love was far, far greater than I had thought. My second daughter was born, and I loved her instantly and equally as much. And the amazing thing is that my love for both of them keeps growing and growing. Now, if I am a limited man, and I can love my children like that, how much more can an unlimited God love His children?

You see, God doesn't love others more than you. You don't have to compete for His love. And you don't have to earn it! We think that we can get more of God's love if only we were better in our behavior. There's Satan's lie again. You are God's child. That sonship means you are the receiver of His great love. It is an unlimited love that you can't alter by doing bad things or good things. You get it all.

So, should I just kick back and enjoy that love? No. There's a little matter of expressing some gratitude. Being God's child and getting all this love makes me feel very free and it makes me want to do things for God. God's love motivates me to do good things because I'm so thankful to Him. As a matter of fact, Paul felt the same thing. He said that it is the love of Christ that controls him (2 Corinthians 5:14). Christ's love, demonstrated by His death for me, is the motivation for me to live for Him. His love drives, or compels, me to want to please Him.

I hope you're getting this. I hope you feel that freedom and motivation, too, because it comes with the territory of *being* God's child. Take a minute and think about it, because there's more.

Not only do you have sonship because you are *born* into God's family but you also have sonship because you are *adopted* into God's family. It's the ultimate double whammy of blessing! You're His child because you chose Him by faith. And you're His child because He chose you by adoption.

"Adoption" is also a technical, theological term in the Bible, and it is a very cool thing. Paul talks about this in the book of Galatians. He tells the believers in Galatia that they were sons (and daughters) by adoption.

> *That is the way it is with us: When we were minors, we were just like slaves ordered around by simple instructions (the tutors and administrators of this world), with no say in the conduct of our own lives.*
>
> *But when the time arrived that was set by God the Father, God sent his Son, born among us of a woman, born under the conditions of the law so that he might redeem those of us who have been kidnapped by the law. Thus we have been set free to experience our rightful heritage. You can tell for sure that you are now fully adopted as his own children because God sent the Spirit of his Son into our lives crying out, "Papa! Father!" Doesn't that privilege of intimate conversation with God make it plain that you are not a slave, but a child? And if you are a child, you're also an heir, with complete access to the inheritance. (Galatians 4:3-7, MSG)*

Adoption gives a person all the rights and privileges of the family that he or she is adopted into. This is done because the parent, out of great love, chooses to give these things. Paul says that because Christ redeemed you (bought you—ownership), He adopts you too. Therefore you are no longer a slave to sin, Satan, and the world. Adoption gives you all the rights of a free person.

The Galatians knew about these things because some of them were once slaves or now owned slaves. During the time when Paul wrote this letter to them, Rome ruled the world. The Romans believed that the people of Rome were far superior to everyone else, so they'd often take slaves to do their labor. Being a slave could range from working for someone to being in chains for hard labor. One thing for sure: a slave had no rights. Slaves could not own property, they could not participate in many of the luxuries of the time, they couldn't go where they wanted to go or do what they wanted to do. If a slave made the master upset, the master could have the slave punished severely or even put to death. Obviously, slaves lived in fear. The only way he or she could be free was to be adopted as the child of a free person.

If a slave was adopted, he or she became part of the family. That person received everything the family received, including the privilege of sharing in the family inheritance. He or she would be called by the adopted family's name and be equal to the children of that family. Adoption was sonship, and sonship was more about privilege than responsibility.

Paul says that God *adopted* you! Because He adopted you, "you are no longer a slave, but a son; and since you are a son, God has made you also an heir" (Galatians 4:7). A lot of students miss the point on this, so follow the logic closely.

I hear Christian high school students say that their life is crummy. They think that because they are Christians (God's children) that God is going to make life boring and no fun—and make them into nerds. And God won't allow them to have really great friends.

That sounds like bondage to me. You are the child of the King of the Universe. He adopted you, and you wear His name. Not only that,

He allows you to be part of the inheritance that He has waiting for His beloved ones. All that He has is yours because, as Paul says, you are an heir. An heir is a person legally entitled to the properties, riches, and assets of the father. An heir is also entitled to the rank that the father has, for example if he is king then the heir has the rank of ruler. So . . . what if you are adopted by the King of the Universe? If you are part of this inheritance, and if God didn't spare His only Son to adopt you, won't He freely give you all good things? Simple logic says that God adopted me *in order to give me good things,* not to make me friendless, boring, mundane, and nerdy.

Sonship means you are part of God's family. He is your Father. He loves you, and nothing can change or alter that. You have His spiritual DNA coursing through your being. You are adopted. You wear His name, which carries great freedom. You are heir to all that is His. You will actually reign with Christ some day: "For if, by the trespass of the one man, death reigned through that one man, how much more will those who receive God's abundant provision of grace and of the gift of righteousness reign in life through the one man, Jesus Christ" (Romans 5:17).

WHOSE I AM IMPLIES PARTNERSHIP

When you enter into a relationship with Jesus Christ you enter into a partnership. That means you share things with Him, you have a special association with Him, and you get to be an active participant in what He is doing. If you are still thinking, then you are realizing that this must come with great privileges too. But it also has its responsibilities.

Let's get one thing out in the open right away about responsibilities to God: They are not meant to generate fear in us. They are meant to draw us into the great things that God is doing. In that sense, the privilege clearly outweighs the responsibility.

Here's how it works. You and I both know that God is doing great things all over the world. He does this daily and has been doing it since the beginning of time. He does great and marvelous things. By being *in Christ* you are allowed to be a part of those great things. God makes you His partner. I don't know about you, but I want to be a partner in something exciting and great that God is doing . . . and the crazy thing is that He lets me. That's quite a privilege and a very cool partnership.

This means that God doesn't *demand* that we tell our friends about Christ. We receive the *privilege* of being the person who tells the story. God is going to do something great in the lives of the people at your school. He is! You can get on that ride and have a firsthand, up close, down and dirty partnership in that great thing, or you can sit back and miss it. God allows you to be His partner, so be it. Being God's partner means that you will always win, even if it doesn't feel like it, or even if you don't see the end result right away.

Peter reminds us that we are not only partners in Christ's inheritance but also in His tough times: "Rejoice that you participate in the sufferings of Christ . . ." (1 Peter 4:13). Ouch! That doesn't sound like fun. It may not be, but it is a whole lot easier to take when we know that the end means we win, because God wins: " . . . so that you may be overjoyed when his glory is revealed" (1 Peter 4:13).

Another way that we are in partnership with God is that we are allowed to imitate God. That's right, *imitate* Him. Consider Ephesians 5:1-2: "Be imitators of God, therefore, as dearly loved children and live a life of love, just as Christ loved us and gave himself up for us as a fragrant offering and sacrifice to God."

Imitating God doesn't mean that I have to pretend to be perfect or that I have to walk on eggshells out of fear that I might do something wrong. The only way I imitate God is in His love. Even then I don't actually reproduce His love; He works through me. I get to be *partners* with God in loving people. It's like I'm going to be the conduit through which His love flows. God is going to pour His love through me into the lives of others. When He is pouring His love through me, I am being like Jesus. I am imitating Christ. This is a fun partnership.

We've looked at several ways we are in partnership with Christ. Let's look at one more: The Bible says that we are partners in a ministry of reconciliation. This means God is making the world right with Himself through Christ's sacrifice on the cross. As He is doing that, He is letting us help by giving us the role of being God's representative to explain what God is already doing. God calls His partners who do this "ambassadors." Here is where Paul explains it:

> *Therefore, if anyone is in Christ, he is a new creation; the old has gone, the new has come! All this is from God, who reconciled us to himself through Christ and gave us the ministry of reconciliation: that God was reconciling the world to himself in Christ, not counting men's sins against them. And he has committed to us the message of reconciliation. We are therefore Christ's ambassadors, as though God were making his appeal through us. We implore you on Christ's behalf: Be reconciled to God. (2 Corinthians 5:17-20)*

An ambassador is a dignitary, a spokesperson, a representative, an honored guest in a foreign place (the list can go on, but you get the idea). That's what God says we are, and that He speaks through us on Christ's behalf to encourage people to be reconciled to Him.

Lots of people thirst for God's love. If you are in this partnership with God, then He is going to let His love flow through you. It will knock people over—as if they were taking a drink from a fire hose. I want to go on this ride!

So many people are afraid that they are going to mess up God's work. Again, that's Satan wanting to rob you of your partnership. The key word is "partner." God isn't just handing things over to you. He isn't taking a hands-off approach. He isn't setting you up to fail. He is still, and always, in control.

I heard a youth pastor tell a youth group one time to imagine standing before God one day . . . "You see all of the other students from your school there too. God opens His books, and your nonChristian friends' names are not there. So those kids have to be cast into hell, into the eternally burning lake of fire. As your friend is being carried away to eternal judgment, that friend may turn to you and say, 'Why didn't you tell me? Why didn't you show me Christ's love?'"

I wanted to stand up and yell: "That will never happen!" Because it's not true. It's not even in the Bible. Romans 1:20 is clear. It says that every person will be without excuse when they stand before God. That means that they will know beyond a shadow of a doubt that they rejected Christ, because God loves them and wants them to have every chance. Nobody will be caught with their pants down, because God is in control. He loves those unsaved friends of ours more than we do. And He will never entrust the eternity of anyone into the hands of a mere mortal. Can you imagine it? God telling people that they have to go to hell because somebody dropped the ball and didn't do the job? What kind of a loving and all-knowing God would entrust the eternity of someone to another sinful human being? That's not loving, nor is it smart.

Jesus did the job. Jesus does the job. The Holy Spirit convicts people of sin and draws them into a relationship with Christ. That's His role, not yours.

But you do get to be His partner in this. Look at it like this. He is drawing these people into a relationship with Himself, and someone is going to get a chance to be His representative, His mouthpiece, His love, His partner. If you don't do it, you'll miss that joyful experience, and He'll give someone else the privilege. He is not willing that anyone should perish, so He's going to hold the reins and let another be His partner in this great adventure. (By the way, you're not going to mess it up, because it's a partnership. That means that He is walking alongside you the whole way.)

When my kids were very little, I would ask them if they wanted to drive the car. "Yes! Yes!" they cried. I'd sit them on my lap, and they would grab the steering wheel, white-knuckling their tiny little fingers. I would then drive around the parking lot, allowing them to steer. They *couldn't* reach the pedals, of course, and the car was never out of my control. They couldn't make a wrong turn because I also had access to the wheel, and I was much more powerful than they were.

They thought they were driving the car. But really, who was driving? My point is simple: I let them be part of a partnership with me, a partnership of driving that car. Partnership with God is like that. Partnership with God doesn't mean that He does His part and then you do your part as a solo act. He partners *through* you. When you look at partnership like that, the privileges far outweigh the responsibilities.

So do you want to drive the car? Think about it.

If you want to stay a Christian in high school,
be absolutely certain WHOSE you are.

THINK IT THROUGH

1. Think about the worst thing you have ever done. Has it made God love you less? Why or why not? What points from this chapter have helped you answer this question?

2. What concept from this chapter most encourages you? Why?

3. What would you tell a Christian friend who feels worthless?

4. How does being a partner with Christ affect your day-to-day life?

5. Do you ever worry about your salvation? What biblical truths in this chapter seem to help?

6. What does it mean to you that "Jesus did the job"? Think: How will this truth affect your life today?

CHAPTER TWO

MARY: AVERAGE GIRL, AWESOME IDENTITY

"I have to talk to you."

"Huh?" He takes a bite of buttered toast. "Hhmm?"

"Really, Dad. It's important."

Hardly looking up, just peeping at her over the morning news-paper, he sips some coffee. "What is it, honey?"

"There was a man in my room last night."

"WHAT!"

Some of the coffee hits the fan.

Jesus told a parable . . .

This man wants to build a house, so he scopes out some construc-tion sites. He sees some land close to the beach, prime property on the rocks of a cliff that overlooks the ocean. He buys the rocky lot and starts to build. He's wise to build it on that solid foundation.

Just days after he starts building, another guy comes along and thinks that he, too, should build a new home. He scopes out the land and decides that he doesn't want to be as far away from the beach as the guy on the rock, so he looks at beachfront property. He finds it right there on the sand. *This will be great,* he thinks. *I can roll right out of bed and be surfing, like, right away.* He didn't stop to think that the foundation under his house was, well, *portable.* Not too wise!

Both men finished their new homes and enjoyed living near the ocean. The guy on the sand would often look up to the cliff and see the man whose house stood there on the rock. He'd think of how much trouble it would have been to build his house up there. Every day, when he wanted to surf, he would have to carry his board down the side of the cliff and then carry it all the way back up when he was done. *Bummer!* he thought. *Way too much trouble. I'd never have any fun! Glad I have this beachfront place.*

The man on the rock would look down from his house and see the guy on the beach surfing and lying in the sun almost every day. Occasionally he'd think, *Maybe that beach guy has it better; looks like he's having a lot of fun down there.* Yet, deep down, the wise man knew that he did the best thing by building his house on that rock.

Now an interesting thing happened to both of them. One night, as they were snug and comfy in their new homes, enjoying a rerun of *Gilligan's Island,* the show was interrupted by an emergency weather report. Hurricane Hezekiah was whipping itself into a frenzy just off the coast. Both men rushed to their windows to check it out. They could see the dark, threatening clouds advancing, laced with lightning flashes. The men raced around, slamming all the doors and storm windows tight.

And then the storm came crashing through like a runaway locomotive. The rain beat loudly, the wind rattled the rafters, and the swell of the ocean sent flood waters swirling around each house. Neither man could hide from this storm. They sat huddled in the corners of their newly built homes.

Then the guy on the sandy beach felt a sudden jolt. *Hey, did the floor just move?* Contemplating that scary question in the semidarkness, he started to feel a cold chill creeping up along his ankles. He looked down and saw his floorboards separating, icy saltwater gushing up through huge cracks. Then another jolt, and a jagged crack opened up across the ceiling and began parting the drywall in the corner. And water—*everywhere!*

Another jolt made the foolish man realize that his nice beachfront house . . . was no longer on the beach. He'd just become the captain of the *Titanic,* and his whole world was sinking. Before he could even think of what to do, his house fell apart and slid, board by board, into the sea.

The wise man? He stayed dry in the corner. In fact, he fell asleep, totally oblivious to the fate of his neighbor. The next morning he woke up to bright sun shining through his window. He stretched and walked outside to survey the storm's damage. He noticed that two shingles had blown off his roof, but as he picked them up off his lawn, he caught a glimpse of his neighbor's beachfront property. The house was gone. The only thing left was the guy's TV, half buried in the sand. The rest of the house was scattered up and down the coast and floating offshore in the surf. Wise man took another look at his own house. Then he stood quietly on his lawn for a long time, occasionally glancing down at those two shingles in his hand.

I think you get the point of Jesus' story: There are two types of people: wise and foolish. You will either be one or the other, and you *choose* which you will be. Both houses in the story are built strong, but they stand on different foundations.

The foundation you build your life upon has to be a firm one, because the storm clouds will form and the rain will fall in every human life. The storm hit both houses with the same smashing intensity. It is going to strike your house too. The outcome will depend on your foundation. Building your life on Christ is the wise response. If you have Christ, you have everything. If you don't have Christ, everything that you have is nothing. Your identity must be built upon the solid rock of Jesus Christ.

As a teenager, you are starting to formulate an identity. This identity will be stretched and shaped and reshaped throughout your life. But why not start the building project right?

But what, exactly, is my identity? you may wonder. It's the core of your character. It is who you are, the person who's still there when everything else is taken away and when nobody sees you. It is shaped by the things you allow yourself to be influenced by, day by day. It is developed by the values you believe in and hold dear. For example, I hear a lot of high schoolers say they are Christians and that they would die for Jesus. Anyone can say that, right? But identity will be tested when the heat is on—meaning that if you say Christ is a value, and that you'll die for Him, *then you certainly will live for Him.* You will deny some things for Him. You will be willing to be embarrassed for Him. Those same ready-to-die students have a more difficult time with that one.

I'm simply saying it's the toughest thing in the world to be a Christian in high school if your identity is sinking its roots into the wrong thing. Let's say you start to build your identity on what you do, like being good at sports, getting excellent grades, honing your artistic talents, working on your looks, or being popular—even things like being the funny guy. You are building on a weak foundation. The storm is brewing.

The foundation needs to be God; otherwise, being a Christian in high school—or anywhere else, for that matter—is impossible. A teenager in the Bible seemed to know all about this. Her identity was rooted in God. Yes, she had to face incredible torrents of wind and rain, a whole town misunderstanding her and thinking she'd blown her life big time. But at the dawn of a new day, her house stood firm.

DEVELOPING A CHRISTIAN IDENTITY

Mary was an average teenage girl. Shortly after she was born, her father began thinking about her marriage. I don't mean he started saving money for the wedding; I mean he was looking for her future husband. The custom of the day was for the father to arrange the marriage of his daughter to a man whose family was of good stock. So Mary's father, from day one, had his eye out for his daughter's perfect mate.

Now she is a teenager, probably about thirteen or fourteen years old. It's old enough to be engaged in that culture, because she's physically able to give birth. By the time Mary reaches fifteen or sixteen, she will be a married woman and maybe even pregnant. That was the custom.

One day Mary strolled home from school with her friends. They were all in the same situation, all being engaged (Mary's fiancé was a young man named Joseph). They spoke together about how much homework they had, about their favorite TV programs, and, of course, about their future husbands.

Mary was excited about her life. Some time earlier, she decided that her identity was going to be in God. She could clearly remember the night that she gave her life to God. She told the Lord that He could have every bit of her. She wanted Him to be in control of her life and to own her. She said she would be willing to do whatever God wanted, wherever He wanted her, and whenever He called. She told God that her time, talents, abilities, skills, and everything that she owned—her body, mind, and spirit—belonged to Him. She was building a solid identity on the most solid of foundations.

Even Mary's way of talking reflected her commitment to God. She had studied Proverbs, one of her favorite books written by one of her relatives, King Solomon. She knew from her study of that book that the things in a person's heart tend to flow out of her mouth. In other words, you talk about the values that shape your identity. It didn't take long in the conversation with her friends before Mary was talking about how she wanted to be the kind of God-honoring woman and wife that Solomon described in his book of wisdom (check it out in Proverbs 31:10-31).

Everyone knew where Mary stood. They admired how she made God the most important value in her life. While most people admired that, some people gave her a hard time for it. In fact, a few made fun of her or challenged her beliefs. A few others were outright cruel to her. They'd play jokes on her or say things that made her feel embarrassed. Despite this, Mary's foundation was secure. She was committed to God. Of course, the storms would come. Her foundation would be tested.

MARY FACES AN IDENTITY TEST

Mary arrived at home and said goodbye to her friends, who continued on to their own homes. As they walked away, she asked them if they were going to youth group that night. They all agreed that they would see each other there.

At youth group, Mary's youth pastor, Rob, spoke about commitment to God. He pointed to Proverbs 20:27 (NASB), which says, "The spirit of man is the lamp of the LORD, searching all the innermost parts of his being." Rob made it clear that God looks at the character of a person and that we will do things based on our character, not just on what we say we will do. He challenged them to be committed enough to God to die for Him.

But Mary knew the real question that would test her identity. It wasn't: "Would you die for God?" Instead, it was: "Will you *live* for Him? Will you really allow Him to have control?" She thought about this often.

When Mary arrived home from youth group, she chatted with her parents, finished some homework that was due the next day, and headed to her room for bed. She was standing in her room, thinking about Rob's talk as she brushed her hair in front of her bedroom mirror. Then, out of the corner of her eye, Mary caught a glimpse of someone standing in the corner.

She turned—it was a man standing there! "Hail favored one," said the man. "The Lord is with you." Needless to say, this freaked Mary out. *What is he talking about, and who is he, and what is he doing in my bedroom?* she thought. She was too scared to scream, and there was no place to run because he was between her and the door. Then the man said, "Don't be afraid, Mary, for you have found favor with God."

This is a lot for Mary to take in. She doesn't know what to think or say, but somehow she feels a peace about the situation. Twice the guy mentioned God, and because he just appeared in her room from out of nowhere, Mary is beginning to think that maybe he is actually a messenger from God. On the other hand: *This is so strange!*

Before Mary could say a word, the messenger told her about a plan God had for her. "First, you're going to have a baby. He's going to be a boy, and you should name him Jesus. He is going to be the Great One, the Son of the Most High God. He will reign over Israel on the throne of David, and His kingdom will be endless and eternal."

When he said this, Mary started to think about what she knew about the Messiah. She'd been taught all her life that Messiah would come someday and maybe this was it. Mary and her friends looked for the coming of Messiah. They didn't know when it would happen, but they were excited about the possibility that it could happen in their lifetime. They all wanted to be ready for His coming too.

When she finally came to the conclusion that this was what this angel was talking about, she must have thought, *this is huge!* But then her mind went back to the first part of the messenger's statement, ". . . you're going to have a baby. . . ."

Whoa, hold up. This is different. This isn't what I signed up for when I said I was going to live for God.

This was a defining point, a test of her identity. Is she really the woman she said she was? God isn't asking her to die for Him; God is asking her to have her entire life turned upside down for Him.

IDENTITY UNDER FIRE

Mary takes a deep breath. There's a small problem here. . . .

"I'm a virgin. How am I supposed to have a baby?" It's an honest question and it's loaded with meaning. Remember, she is engaged to a man named Joseph. Their families have arranged this marriage and have planned a great wedding to unite their families.

Her question is not just about sex. Mary knows how conception works; that's the easy part. She is admitting that she and Joseph weren't sexually active, but she also knew that if this child was the Son of the Most High, then Joseph wouldn't be the one getting her pregnant. This was going to be confusing!

However, the heavenly messenger tells her that the Holy Spirit and the power of God will come upon her, and God will impregnate her. Since God is the Creator of everything and therefore in control of conception anyway, this may be weird, but wasn't too far a stretch for Mary to understand.

The hard part was what Mary may be implying in her question. Mary knew that she was being asked to do something difficult. I think her question is more about the radical change that her life is going to take on as the result of this awesome message unfolding in the coming days.

I believe Mary was thinking through her identity in God. Imagine this. *Okay, I'm going to be a pregnant teenager. How am I going to explain this to my parents tomorrow?*

Can you see it? Mary has this vision of coming down for breakfast. Her dad is sitting at the kitchen table reading the morning paper. Mary timidly sits down and doesn't say a word, at least for a while. But she knows that, eventually, she has to say something.

"Dad, I have to talk to you."

"Huh?"

"Really, Dad. It's important."

"What is it, honey?"

"Ummm. Well. There was a man in my room last night."

"What!" he yells as he crumples the newspaper.

"Wait, Dad. It was an angel, it was an angel, so calm down!"

"What do you mean, *angel*? If there was a guy in your room last night . . . you better be telling me the truth, young lady, or you'll be grounded till you're thirty!" Dad's coffee has spilled on the tablecloth and sloshed on his shirt.

"Really, Dad, I'm telling the truth! He said he had a message for me from God and then . . . he was gone. He was only there for a couple minutes."

"Okay, Mary, what's going on here? An angel with a message from God, huh? Any chance you were just dreaming? Because now I'm think-ing: What would God have to say to you that's so important I have to ruin my tie the next morning?" Dad resorts to his standard ironic humor that's not so funny. He still seems frustrated and wary, but there's some relief in his tone too. A silly little dream would explain everything.

Mary pauses for a moment. "He said, Dad, that Messiah is coming."

Her dad chuckles, quite relieved now. "Oh, that's good, Mary, real good. See, I'm trying to read the paper here. And we all know that Messiah is coming soon . . . ha, ha . . . you kids, always dreaming and joking around."

After a long pause Mary breaks the silence again. "Dad . . . there's more. I'm pregnant."

She grabs her books and runs toward the door, hoping that he didn't really hear it, and that maybe she could get out of the house before whatever he did hear sinks in.

Instead, the predictable paternal freak-out begins. "What? . . . Stop! . . . You! . . . What! . . . *Pregnant?*"

It's as if every molecule in her dad's body has come unglued. He is out of his seat, pacing, folding and unfolding the paper, kicking at little things on the floor. His face turns several shades of red, and the veins in his forehead look as if they might explode at any moment.

"I'm gonna *kill* that Joseph!"

"No, Dad! It's not Joseph. It was God!"

At this point, Mary is pretty sure: *My parents are never going to believe this. Never! God supernaturally got me pregnant? Who's going to believe that? They'll be so hurt. The more I try to explain, the more they'll think I'm just trying to protect Joseph—or some guy they conjure up in their own minds.*

What am I going to do?

After all, there aren't any cases where God impregnates anyone in the rest of Scripture. It's not like God has done this before. Mary is risking huge rejection from her family on this one. She may have to watch them be incredibly hurt, with no way to relieve their pain. She may have to live the rest of her life alone. She keeps asking: "How can this be?"

At that moment Mary had to check who she was. *Am I really God's? Is that where my identity really lies?* She knew that her identity could not be built on the foundation of making her parents happy or on what her family thought of her. It needed to be built on God. If she would die for God, she certainly could be rejected and lonely for Him.

Just then she had two more scary thoughts. First, of course, she was mortified over what Joseph was going to think. *Oh! He'll be so hurt and angry. There goes our life together!*

Then, on the heels of that envisioned disaster, came more implications: *What's everyone else going to think? The gossip's going to be flying* — *all over church, all over school, all over town.*

"Did you hear? Little Mary is pregnant!"

"No! Really? And she was such a sweet girl!"

"I guess all that talk about commitment to God was just talk."

"Huh, I never would've thought she was living some kind of double life! I'm surprised at Joseph too."

"Oh, no, Joseph isn't the father."

"He's not?"

"Uh, nobody knows who the real father is. But get this: Mary says God did it."

Whoa!

Raised eyebrows. Snickering faces. Gossip in the school hallways. Apparently, little Mary has flipped out.

People just aren't going to understand, Mary thinks. She knew this was going to have some bad repercussions. The people around her would probably be judgmental. Maybe even the people at her church would be condemning. And, of course, some of the church parents would forbid their kids from hanging out with Mary. Can you hear them? "You are not hanging out with that Mary girl. She's promiscuous and deceitful, and I will not have my son or daughter being influenced by her."

Mary wasn't stupid. She knew this might cost her some friendships. She also knew she'd have to suffer the condemnation of people who wouldn't understand and who needed to feel morally superior.

If Mary's identity was built on the foundation of popularity and being liked by everyone, then that foundation would be shifting in a few days, and Mary's house would fall. But Mary belonged to God. Her identity was founded on the Rock. She knew that she was facing a great and terrible storm; raindrops were hitting her face already! But if she would die for Him, then she certainly could be judged wrongly, be condemned, and suffer for Him. *But I don't understand it, and it's definitely not going to be any fun. How can this be?*

Another quick scene may have burst into Mary's mind. She's at school. Not only is she going to suffer ridicule there from her peers— especially the ones who have always been particularly cruel—but she will have to give some things up.

GIVING UP THE OTHER IDENTITY

What will happen when she starts to show, you know, look pregnant? No more cute clothes, and that's probably the least of her problems. She won't be able to sit all day listening to lectures. She'll be as big as a house. School desks aren't really built for pregnant girls.

What if she gets morning sickness? She may miss a lot of classes; she may have to leave in the *middle* of a lot of classes. And what about the volleyball team? She'll have to quit that (a pregnant setter just doesn't do the job very well). She may have to give up her entire extra-curricular life, like her part-time job at the market.

Yes, pregnancy is going to take a toll on her body. She'll be huge and she'll be tired. She'll have all that water weight, back pain, and maybe a little tooth decay. She won't be able to stand for long in the market during the afternoons (and, anyway, the way the rumor mill is churning out the hot news, her boss may have to let her go for fear of losing business).

Mary knows how hard she works at studying, and staying in shape, and all the other things in a teenager's life that demand discipline. She's sure it won't be easy to give these things up for the disciplines that come with being a new mom. She'll have a baby. High school life would come to a dramatic end because she'll be planning life around feedings, changing diapers, and frequent naps. Her friends will be planning life around homecoming, ACT tests, and prom. She becomes overwhelmed with the thought of all this, so she asks: "How can this be?"

As Mary imagines her life without school, volleyball, cute clothes, and being in shape, she probably has less of a difficult time with the thought of giving things up than with the idea of breaking up with Joseph, hurting her parents, or being rejected by her friends. After all, she can give things up for God. It will be difficult, but her identity isn't built on things; it's built on God. Mary won't let the style of her clothes, her friends' opinions, her intelligence, or her talents define who she is. She is God's. She knows that if she has God she has everything; if she has everything but doesn't have God, then she has nothing. *I can give up everything for you, God!* Then, because it's the season of scary thoughts in her life, her mind turns once again to the horrible fear that's been there from the beginning of the strange events . . . Joseph! *Can I really give up Joseph, the love of my life? What will I tell him?*

Although this marriage was arranged, she had grown to love Joseph very much, and he loved her too. She and Joseph were getting excited about the wedding. They had talked on the phone almost every night, planning the celebration and all the joy to follow in their future life together. *This is going to be a great blow to his spirit,* Mary thinks. Like all the other people in her life, she imagined that Joseph probably wouldn't believe that the Holy Spirit did this to her. It sounded so sensational, so "out there." She imagines the conversation. . . .

Joseph is crying uncontrollably, as is she. "Mary, tell me the truth. I need to know, I *deserve* to know who you were with."

"Joseph, I *am* telling you the truth."

"I don't know if I can handle this." He turns to the door, his shoulders shuddering with his sobs. "I have to leave. I can't be here with you." He walks out the door.

Mary imagines it will be the last time she'll see Joseph. She can't predict how he will react to her story. He may become so angry that he'll never want to see her again. He may feel so humiliated that he'll move out of town, far away, where nobody knows him. Or he may feel so deeply hurt that he becomes physically ill or depressed to the point of suicide.

No matter how she looks at it, Mary must consider losing Joseph. God wouldn't ask her to do something that could totally destroy her entire life. He wouldn't ask her to give up everything, including the treasure that she thought He brought to her. Mary knows that if she has God, she has everything. *But this one is so hard to understand!*

She remembers reading about Job in her Bible, the man who said he would trust in the Lord even if he thought it would destroy him. Job's identity was embedded in God. When the storm hit Job, and things were at the worst of the worst, Job concluded that "though he slay me, yet will I hope in him" (Job 13:15).

Mary knew that this pregnancy would not only affect her but it would affect other people too, particularly Joseph. Mary knew that her identity could not rest in her relationships. She knew that God had given her Joseph, and she came to the conclusion that God could also take him away. She knew she had to be content with God. If her identity was built upon the foundation of a human relationship, then her life would fall apart if that relationship were to go away.

It will hurt so much if Joseph leaves me! But if I have God, then I have everything.

SETTLING INTO HER SECURE IDENTITY

Mary's identity was built on the solid foundation of God even though it was so hard to understand God's plan. "How can this be?" she asks.

The angel answers by telling her that nothing is impossible for God. I'm sure Mary knew that in her *mind*. But now it must have truly resonated within her *identity*. At that moment she realized she belonged to God; she existed to bring God glory. She realized that God's plan was perfect, and that He would be in control of this impossible situation.

Mary likely recalled a story she'd heard in church about her ancestor, father Abraham. God told him that his wife, Sarah (who was over ninety years old), was going to have a baby, just like He did with Mary. This baby was going to start the nation of Israel. Abraham hears this, looks at his elderly wife, and asks the same question Mary asks: "How can this be?"

Now it would be important to note here that Abraham's question *was* a sex question. He knew his wife couldn't have children anymore. Sarah hears that she is going to be a ninety-year-old pregnant woman, and she laughs. *Ridiculous!* But the answer that comes back to Abraham is the same answer given to Mary: "Nothing is impossible with God."

Wow! It's déjà vu *all over again,* Mary thinks. She knows God did the impossible in that situation; she's living proof of His ability. Sarah and Abraham had Isaac, who had Jacob, who had twelve sons, who became the tribes of the nation of Israel, just as God promised. Mary came from the tribe of Judah. She was alive because nothing was impossible for God. That thought must have made Mary's identity even more secure.

Mary realizes that with God she has everything. With God nothing is impossible. She knows she is created for His pleasure, so she answers the angel by saying, "I am the Lord's servant. May it be to me as you have said" (see Luke 1:38). She gave herself totally to God, her identity built completely upon Him.

IDENTITY CHECK – WHAT ABOUT *YOU*?

Now we come down to the identity of a very important person: you. Are you convinced that if you're going to be a Christian in high school, your identity must rest upon a solid foundation? Can you follow in the footsteps of Mary, and let her example be your guide?

It won't be easy. Remember that Mary was ready to lose her family, friends, and fiancé. She knew that if she would die for God then she could also suffer for Him, or be lonely, or be judged and wrongly condemned for Him. She knew she was secure, even if she was rejected or if her reputation was slandered. Her life and identity were built on God.

When Mary says, "May it be to me as you have said," she is agreeing to be part of God's plan. She is willfully lining up her identity with her will. On the other hand, what if Mary had said, "I have some problems with this, so I think I'm going to pass on the pregnant thing this time"? She would have missed a great ride that God was going to take her on. After all, God would send Messiah into the world, with or without Mary.

What if Mary had said, "I'd love to be the mother of Messiah, but can we talk about some of the details? Can you wait until I graduate? Or, if that's not convenient, can you at least wait until volleyball season is over?" If that were Mary's attitude, then God may have given this awesome opportunity to some other girl. However, Mary thought it through and, because her identity was rooted in God, she pulled the trigger and decided that God far outweighed anything she would encounter.

She knew that the storm would indeed come, but her identity was built on God and nothing else. Her statement shows that she agrees to be God's woman in this plan. But here's the neat part: After she agrees, *Mary realizes that she will be blessed among all women throughout the ages.* Just listen to the thrill in her voice as she lifts her heart in gratitude and praise to God:

> *My soul glorifies the Lord*
> *and my spirit rejoices in God my Savior,*
> *for he has been mindful of the humble state of his servant.*
> *From now on all generations will call me blessed,*
> *for the Mighty One has done great things for me — holy*
> *is his name.*
> *His mercy extends to those who fear him, from generation*
> *to generation.*
> *He has performed mighty deeds with his arm; he has scat-*
> *tered those who are proud in their inmost thoughts.*
> *He has brought down rulers from their thrones but has*
> *lifted up the humble.*

He has filled the hungry with good things but has sent the
rich away empty.

He has helped his servant Israel, remembering to be merci-
ful to Abraham and his descendants forever, even as he said to
our fathers. (Luke 1:46-55)

She says that her soul glorifies the Lord. All that she is exists for
God's glory. In other words, the only reason she's alive is so God will
be praised and honored through her life.

Isn't that an amazing way to live? Do you know that is the same
reason you exist? Yes, you were created for the same purpose. God
made you for His glory. You *are* (that's your identity), because of Him.

Your identity is the real you, the person you are when nobody sees
you. And you can't have two identities. You can't be one person at
church and another person at school (one of those so-called identities
will be a fake). You can't turn an identity on or off. Your identity shines
through in the decisions you make, the attitudes you express, and the
words you speak. Mary's identity was consistent. It permeated her
thoughts, decisions, and actions.

Being identified as a Christian supersedes being a son or daughter, a
friend, a star, a good student, an employee, or any other role you play. If
you want to be a Christian in high school, you have to make Jesus the foundation of who you are. Invite Him to be in control of every part of you—
your heart, body, and mind. Understand that you exist for His pleasure.

Think about it! It makes wise sense to say that anything that can
fade away, be taken away, or can change, is not a very solid foundation.
The only thing that will last forever is Jesus. Will you build your identity on that lasting foundation?

If you want to be a Christian in high school,
you can't turn an identity on or off; make Jesus the
foundation of who you are.

THINK IT THROUGH

1. When have you been the most misunderstood? How did you cope with the feelings?

2. In your opinion, is it harder to die for God or to live for Him? Why?

3. How has God rearranged your plans for life? High school? Are there things you had to give up in order to maintain your identity as a believer? If so, what were they?

4. Read the parable of the two builders in Matthew 7:24-27. Name some of the things upon which teens today build their identities. Which are most tempting to you?

5. How can you tell when someone is secure in his or her identity? What are some of the practical signs?

6. Are you secure in your identity as a Christian in high school? What are some of the things that allow you to be secure in living your faith?

7. If one of your friends made fun of your beliefs during a classroom discussion, how would you respond to him or her? What would make you respond that way?

CHAPTER THREE

DANIEL: NOT UNDER THE INFLUENCE

Azariah grabs one of the pool cues and starts racking up the table. "Can you believe how cool this place is?"

"Yeah, man," says Hananiah, plopping down on the over-stuffed sofa. "I could definitely get used to it here. . . . Hey, where's the remote?"

"Sure is great," Daniel says. "Did you see the workout center, Jacuzzi, and swimming pool downstairs when we came in?"

"Boy, that food sure smells good too!"

"Ah . . . but the Law of Moses says we can't eat that stuff."

"We can taste it, can't we, Mr. Holier-than-Thou Boy? Is that really eating? Come on!"

Your world is influencing you. Have you noticed? It's trying to shape you into what it wants you to be. That influence can creep in under the radar because it's so subtle. Slowly but surely, you start to become what the world wants you to be instead of what God wants you to be. Yet I've never met a kid who says:

"I woke up one morning and chose to start a drug habit."
"One day I just made up my mind that I'd be an alcoholic."
"Last night I decided that I should get pregnant."
"On that beautiful afternoon, I figured life was just too good."

Nobody says: "Today, I think I'll destroy my life." On the contrary, every deep-in-trouble kid I've ever met tells me the big mess they're facing was never the plan. They just didn't think it could happen to them.

The apostle Paul offers a solution: "Do not conform any longer to the pattern of this world, but be transformed by the renewing of your mind. Then you will be able to test and approve what God's will is — his good, pleasing and perfect will" (Romans 12:2). Yet a lot of kids do let the world slowly conform them until they end up not being the person they wanted to be. The big things happen as a result of a person being shaped by all the little, seemingly less-harmful influences. Many times these influences come in the form of peer influence. This is commonly called "peer pressure," but be real — nobody pressures you into doing anything. You choose to do the thing you do. Peer influence can interfere with being a Christian in high school, and it all starts with your mind. So . . . will God be in control of your thinking?

One teenager, Daniel, really had to work hard at this. Let me give you a little background. When Daniel was about fourteen or fifteen years old Nebuchadnezzar ruled Babylon, the country just east of Daniel's nation of Israel. Nebuchadnezzar had big plans — to rule the entire world — so he started with the countries surrounding Babylon. Naturally, Israel was on his hit list.

Try to imagine this. Daniel is sitting in freshman algebra class at school one day. Suddenly the doors burst open and Nebuchadnezzar's soldiers come crashing in, armed and intimidating. They announce: "Israel now belongs to Babylon. Hail to the king!" They look around the room and spot Daniel along with a few other popular, good-looking kids. "Come with us!" they yell, hustling them out of the classroom. The next thing he knows, Daniel is whisked back to Babylon as a hostage, probably thinking, *Will I ever see my family again?*

History tells us that Nebuchadnezzar approached expanding his kingdom with brains as well as brawn. Whenever he took over a nation, he'd first establish military command, then he would take the most promising teenagers as hostages. He would take the teenagers for two reasons. First, if he had the best teenagers, that nation wouldn't fight back for fear of killing their own children. Second, he could train them to be his ambassadors and send them back to their country after he made peace. They would then become his governors in their own country. So, in old Neb's master plan of world domination, this teen-taking approach was a great method of subduing nations.

FOLLOW THE POPULAR CROWD

Daniel is scared. He doesn't know what these soldiers have in mind when they take him hostage. *Are we going to be dirty, starving slaves forever? Will we be taken out and have our heads lifted from our bodies—or worse?* Not happy thoughts! Daniel and his friends are not yet aware of "the royal plan." When Daniel is pushed outside the building, he sees a number of the smart or athletic kids from his school—and from all over the city and nation—being rounded up. What an elite crowd of hostages! Daniel 1:3-4 (NASB) tells us about this group:

> *The king ordered Ashpenaz, the chief of his officials, to bring in some of the sons of Israel, including some of the royal family and of the nobles, youths in whom was no defect, who were good-looking, showing intelligence in every branch of wisdom, endowed with understanding, and discerning knowledge, and who had ability for serving in the king's court; and he ordered him to teach them the literature and language of the Chaldeans.*

Obviously, Nebuchadnezzar had high standards for hostages. Daniel is with the best of the best. These kids were hot, smart, athletic, and well-dressed. They were leaders, probably the captains of all the school sports teams or on student council—all those naturally talented kids everyone looks up to. They were important, too, because their parents were influential people and probably wealthy. Yes, these kids made up the who's who among teens in Israel.

Nebuchadnezzar wanted these students to be trained and receive the best education in Babylonian ways. His plan was to give them the very best, treat them like royalty, and then establish them as his governors throughout the world, especially in their own country. And he wins them over by giving them the best of everything. Therefore, when they return home as the new mayors of their towns, they'll convince the citizens that good old Neb is really a great guy. Hey, they are living proof!

One by one, each student appears before a high-ranking officer named Ashpenaz. He looks them over and tells them the king's plan. They are going to study at Babylon Gardens Prep, an elite private school downtown. They'll train as ambassadors, learn from all the great books of the world, eat the best food, strengthen their bodies through all kinds of recreational activities. "Guys, it's all good," says Ashpenaz. "So go along with the king's wonderful plan for you, or . . . be killed."

Tough call? The way Ashpenaz would put it is: "You have one of two choices, either you live like a king in the coming days, or you die now."

A no-brainer, right? But Daniel must have thought, *There must be some catch. Where's the fine print on this contract?*

Then Ashpenaz came out with it. "Mighty King Nebuchadnezzar is a man of his word. He does in fact desire to make you an ambassador of the nation of Babylon, provided that you study hard and don't resist (you'll like it too much to resist anyway)."

How would you feel if you heard this? Some of the teens didn't believe it. Some of them felt relieved. But all of them still harbored a certain amount of fear and distrust in their hearts.

They start their long trip to Babylon. On their way, the guards are telling them that Nebuchadnezzar's plan is for real.

"You punk kids get to be ambassadors and governors in a few years," one says.

"You better watch how you talk to these kids," another yells. "You might be taking orders from them soon."

"Yeah, King Nebbie is gonna give you guys the best of everything. My kids should have it so good," another chimes in.

Over and over on this long trip to Babylon they hear about why they are hostages. The more they hear, the more convinced they become. *Suppose it's true? Wow! Me—a big-time ruler!*

When they get to Babylon, the king himself greets them. "It's all true," he says. "You will be my ambassadors to the world. I will make you powerful young men and women." Daniel looks around at this popular and elite group. In some ways he feels great because these are the coolest kids he knows. Yet he still doesn't quite trust Nebuchadnezzar, and that makes him cautious. Some of his friends, though, are starting to love this idea. All of them, including Daniel, have heard of Nebuchadnezzar's extravagant methods of training his ambassadors, and many of the hostages start to express their delight in these arrangements.

"Hey, this is great!" one student says. "We're on our own."

"I can't believe it, no parents or teachers telling us what to do," says another.

"It's kind of like camp, only better—we're totally independent."

Keep on imagining. Nebuchadnezzar tells them they're going to have the best of everything. He arranges for them to live in the brand-new, five-star Babylonian Hilton Tower Hotel while attending the prep school. Each of them can pick his own roommate. "You'll have a personal butler and maid for each room. Once you get settled in, the butler will take you to the mall where you can buy new clothes, whatever you want; money is no object. After all, we want you to look the best because we think you *are* the best."

Daniel and his friends start to think it's sounding too good to be true. Nebuchadnezzar reminds them that he really is a great guy and that they are in governor's training school. Slowly but surely this truth starts sinking in. They begin enjoying their new life.

The king tells them they'll be assigned a personal tutor to meet with them every day. That tutor will train them in the customs and language of the Chaldeans (the people of Babylon). "Your tutor will be your main teacher for the next three years. At the end of the three years, there will be a final exam. If you pass, you will enter into my personal service as a governor."

Daniel and the gang started to realize that this guy and this new life was for real. He meant what he said. He really respected them. He was giving them the best of everything. *Maybe this hostage thing isn't such a bad deal, after all.*

GETTING SO, SO COMFORTABLE

Daniel and his friend Azariah decide they're going to be roommates. They arrive at the Babylon Hilton and find that their room (like everyone else's) is a huge connecting suite. They walk through the doors of their suite and into a luxury living area, complete with cable TV, computer, state-of-the-art surround sound CD and DVD, Xbox, pool table—and a refrigerator loaded with great stuff to eat. While Daniel and Azariah are swooning over how cool this place is, their friends Hananiah and Mishael come walking out of the joining bedroom.

"Hey, we're suite-mates!" Mishael yells.

"Can you believe how cool this place is?" Azariah says as he grabs one of the pool cues and starts racking up the table.

"Yeah, man," says Hananiah, plopping down on the overstuffed sofa. "I could definitely get used to it here."

The excitement was high. Everybody was running through the halls of the hotel checking out each other's rooms. This went on all night, and nobody came around to tell them they had to be quiet or they had a curfew time for "lights out." *Maybe Old Neb is going to be true to his word—what a great opportunity for us!*

The next morning the teens get up and come down to the lobby where they are escorted to a great dining room. Nebuchadnezzar and Ashpenaz are there to greet them. They open the doors of this awesome dining hall and reveal tables loaded with food; the best food— gourmet food. It smells so great, and looks so good, that everyone rushes into the hall and starts chowing down. It was a feast fit for a king . . . or at least a bunch of junior ambassadors in training.

How would you be feeling right about now? Just think of it. You are far away from home. Your parents aren't there to always look over your shoulder. You're living in the most outrageous place you can imagine with a bunch of your old friends and a whole lot of new friends, all of whom are the hottest-looking, smartest, coolest, most popular teenagers from all over your country. The "best of the best," as they say.

Do you think you'd try to live right? Would you make sure you still obeyed your curfew, even if your folks weren't there to check up on you? Would you still clean up after yourself, even though you knew you had a maid? Do you think your attitudes would change? Do you think you would drop your guard a little on some of the rules and regulations that you knew were right? Would you compromise your standards if your friends started to compromise theirs? Well that's what happened to the kids of Israel.

You see, the Law of Moses (the first five books of the Bible) said certain foods were okay, but other foods were definitely off the menu—like pork or shellfish. So . . . when Nebuchadnezzar passed them the nice, crisp bacon or the luscious, creamy clam chowder, should they turn up their noses? *But how is the king going to feel about that— me acting like an ungrateful little snob?*

As it turned out, Nebuchadnezzar's world started to squeeze them into its mold. Can't you just hear the conversation at the dinner table?

"The Law says that we shouldn't eat this stuff, guys."

"We can just taste it, can't we?"

"Well . . . I guess it's just food, a little thing. No big deal."

"And why upset the king over a little piece of shrimp? . . . Have you tried the cocktail sauce yet, Dan? Awesome!"

They try it . . . and they like it. One by one the teens start to see that those who are eating are "having fun." Not only was Neb's world squeezing them into a mold, but the peer pressure was kicking in too. You and I both know the plan, because we've BTDT (been there, done that). They rationalize that it wouldn't hurt to do it too, and the next thing they know, they've compromised on a "little thing."

BEWARE OF THE LITTLE THINGS

Even the smallest compromises are dangerous. You see, they tend to lead to more and more compromise — and we end up with a big problem down the road.

Maybe you're realizing that you need to look at some of the little things in your own life these days. If you want to be a Christian in high school, you have to avoid the compromises. Some of those little things include how you dress, how you treat teachers and parents, how you talk when you're with friends.

Of course, I'm not writing in order to tell you what to *do*; I'm hoping to help you *think*. You already know when you're doing something that isn't right, because as a Christian you have the Holy Spirit living within you. He convicts you of right and wrong. He's the one who reveals your motives. And in the middle of all the issues you face, each day, He is renewing your mind.

Emily came into my office because she was mad at her parents. "They are so out of date and conservative," she said. "They don't want me to wear some of the shirts I bought at the mall. They say the shirts are too tight and they don't like it that my belly shows. It's no big deal; that's the style today," she said.

"Even if it is the style, Emily, should you be wearing it?" I asked.

"It's not a sexual thing," she said.

"You're right, it's an obedience thing," I replied. "You need to obey your parents regardless of the issue."

A few weeks later, Emily's mom met with me to tell me that Emily was grounded and that she couldn't come to the amusement park trip planned for that weekend. Apparently, Emily had told her parents she was taking the shirts back.

But she didn't.

Instead, Emily brought the shirts to school and kept them in her locker. She would go to school dressed to please her parents. But once she arrived at school, she'd change into the other "cool" clothes.

One day her mom walked into a fast-food place with some of her friends for lunch. Emily happened to be there with school friends—wearing the clothes her mom thought were back on the store shelves. Emily's actions had gotten her into deeper water, because now she had to work on regaining her parents' trust along with facing the consequences of disobedience. Emily just didn't *think*. What had been a little compromising issue turned into a bigger trust issue.

BE TRANSFORMED, NOT CONFORMED

Let's get back to Daniel. When the guys returned to their suite, Daniel had a talk with his friends. He might have said, "Guys, this isn't right. We can't eat that food. It just isn't honoring to God."

"You're right," says Mishael. "But the food looks and smells so good . . . do you really think it matters?"

"Even if it doesn't matter, we have to put God first and obey Him."

"Well, what should we do?" Azariah asks.

"I'm not sure yet," Daniel says. "But shouldn't we at least pray for wisdom?"

The next morning when they wake up Daniel meets the guys in the living room of their suite and tells them about an idea he has. They should ask whether they can eat only the things their Bible allows.

"What if they won't let us?" Hananiah asks.

"Well, we have to stick together and just keep praying and do the right thing, even if they won't let us." If you read the biblical story in Daniel 1, Daniel does ask Ashpenaz if they can be exempt from eating the king's food. And Ashpenaz says, "No."

Then God gives Daniel wisdom, He renews Daniel's mind, and the young man comes up with a plan. "What if you give us ten days to eat the food that we want," Daniel challenges, "and at the end of the ten days, you could test us to see whether we're just as healthy and strong as the rest of the group? If we aren't, then make a decision about what we should do. If we are actually healthier, then let us stick to the plan and eat the food that our Law allows us to eat."

Ashpenaz thought this was a good idea, so he agreed. At the end of the ten-day time limit, Daniel, Hananiah, Azariah, and Mishael all looked (and were) healthier and stronger than any other kid. Ashpenaz let them stay on their diet, and they remained faithful to God.

The pressure and influence on Daniel was no greater than the pressure and influences on you today. In fact, the influence of their peers may have been even stronger than some of the influences you may face today. They were in a situation that allowed for much more compromise, because the controllers were gone. When they came to that dining room every day, their friends were eating whatever they wanted while Daniel and the guys were being served different food. I'm sure Daniel was seen as a troublemaker and even got teased or ridiculed.

"Look! This kid thinks hot dogs are bad for you. What's the matter, Daniel, too anal to eat something with flavor?"

"Hey, Daniel, you afraid your mommy's gonna catch you eating something you shouldn't?"

"I can't believe that you think God is gonna get all bent out of shape because you ate a little bacon bit! You're so lame, Danny-boy!"

"My, my! This ham steak is deee-licious. Want a little bite to go with your tofu casserole, Danster? Ha! What a bunch of losers!"

"I guess those Kosher Kids think they're too good for us — can't even sit at the same table. Well, forget about them!"

I'm sure Mishael and Hananiah got sucked into a lot of debates about why they weren't eating the rich food. I'm sure that Azariah fought plenty of internal battles, because it was easy to rationalize that this was just a little thing. It's no different today, is it? Daniel and his three friends felt the influence of the other so-called friends, just as you do. These were normal teenagers with normal teenage desires. But can you really be a Christian in high school without refusing, at some point, to conform to the world's standards?

INFLUENCER, OR JUST INFLUENCED?

Here's the Big Question you can be asking yourself: *How can I be an influencer in my world instead of just being the influenced one?* I'm going to suggest five responses—ways you can prepare yourself for the inevitable onslaught of questionable influences.

1. Make up your mind . . . way up front. It starts with a look at Daniel 1:8: "Daniel resolved not to defile himself with the royal food and wine." I love that verse. Daniel resolved, made up his mind, came to a conscious decision ahead of time. If you want to be a Christian in high school you have to scope out the land mines in the pathway ahead of you, and make up your mind to step around them. Remember Romans 12; it's all about your making up your mind to be God-honoring—and God continuing to renew your mind with His thinking. Daniel determined that he wasn't going to be molded into the man Nebuchadnezzar wanted; instead, he'd be molded into the man God wanted. Even if the issue at hand seemed to be "a little thing."

What do you have to make up your mind about? John, a sophomore, told me he is in a not-so-good relationship with a girl, and that it's keeping him from growing closer to the Lord. I was curious to find out why it was doing that (because I often think we blame our spiritual problems on others). John said that he and his girlfriend kept "getting way too physical." He said that they just started out with little things, but then they started doing more and more things that were getting out of control. I asked him if he had talked with her about it. "Yes," he said. "But she doesn't think there's any problem at all; she figures things are going along just fine. But I feel like I'm compromising more and more."

John went on to say that he'd prayed about it and feels that he should break up. "So why don't you do that?" I asked.

"I can't, because I keep going back and forth between breaking up and not breaking up. Sometimes I think it's not that big a deal because we haven't gone all the way yet. Other times, I'm pretty sure God isn't pleased with this relationship."

My advice to John was that he do what Daniel did. Make up your mind; set your will to do this; purpose in your heart to do the right thing. John decided to break off the relationship that night. And yes, it was tough to do. But he followed the Lord on that issue.

God may or may not be leading you to change your relationships. But if He is, it might be hard to do. Regardless of what the compromising issue is, it may be very hard to do. That's the test. Will you make up your mind to be faithful to Him? Will you resolve in your heart to do what He wants, ahead of time?

2. *Keep making the judgment call: Who's the strongest here?* When you're with certain people, it's as if you are on the seesaw of influence. You have to decide whether your own strength of character and the biblical values that you buy into as a Christian are going to outweigh theirs. Who is going to end up influencing whom?

In other words, as you enter into each situation and relationship, scope it out and ask yourself: *Over the long haul, who's likely to win the battle of influence here?* If the influences around you are stronger than the influence that God wants to have on you, then you're in trouble.

God calls His children to be lights in the darkness. That means you don't avoid the darkness, the world around you. It means that you become a stronger influence than the world around you. If you can't be a stronger influence on your nonChristian friends, then you should rethink your desire to constantly hang out with them. Daniel had three godly friends that he surrounded himself with. If you read through the book of Daniel you'll see that they prayed for each other and stood up together for what was right. They were friends who influenced each other for God.

3. *Choose your friends wisely.* Obvious, right? If you want to be a Christian in high school you have to surround yourself with friends who love Jesus and want to please Him. Read that last sentence again. I didn't say surround yourself with a lot of Christians. Sadly, a lot of Christian teenagers demonstrate by their attitudes and actions that loving and pleasing Jesus is hardly a priority. Just because a person is a Christian doesn't mean he or she will be a good influence on you.

Many times I hear teens say that they wish they could go to a Christian school because of the better influences there. And it's true that the curriculum and teachers will be geared toward a more ethical or biblical worldview. But the truth: The same stuff that happens in a public high school happens in a Christian high school. I've talked to countless kids who say their language is worse with their Christian friends, or that they got drunk with their Christian friends, or that they lost their virginity with their Christian boyfriend or girlfriend.

The Bible doesn't distinguish between Christian or nonChristian surrounding this issue of influencers. It says: "Do not be misled: 'Bad company corrupts good character'" (1 Corinthians 15:33). If the company you keep exercises a bad influence over you, then it isn't good. Look at that verse again. It also implies that if you are not exercising a good influence over your friends, then *you* are bad company, and you're deceived.

4. *Become an expert at discernment—how to tell whether your friends are a bad influence on you.* Here's the key: You know it when you exercise good

influence on people. Daniel and his friends prayed together. Ask your friends to pray with you about the influences you have and are controlled by. Pray with your friends about the things you struggle with. If your friends think it's too weird for you to pray together, then start looking for some Christian friends who will be a better influence over you.

Daniel and his friends were young men of prayer. That helped them stay strong and exercise good influence over each other. When the heat was on, they were all on the same page. They all had the same values and convictions. They all had the same desires and passions. They were all thinking the same things, because God was renewing their minds.

And don't be deceived—if you are not in a strong place with God, you can't change your friend, whose bad influence is working overtime. You must first be in a place where there is a strong, God-honoring influence on you.

In my own life, I recall three guys in my youth group who grew up together from birth. They went to the same school and became great friends. When they got to junior high they started to develop different desires. The world was beginning to squeeze them into its mold. I confronted one of the guys in the hallway between classes and pointed out how strong they could be if they came together to pray for each other. "That's too weird," he said. "We've never done anything like that."

"Well, how about trying?" I said.

"I don't know—like what should I say to them—'Hey, wanna get religious?'" he said sarcastically.

"Sure, that could work," I said. "But it could be better if you said that you think your friendship could be stronger and you think that you could be a powerful influence on your school, church, and friends if you began praying together."

"Okay, that sounds cool."

"But I think you also have to have a plan too."

"Like what?" He looked puzzled while trying to avoid the kids pushing past him between the lockers.

"Well, when are you going to do this, how often, where will you meet? That kind of plan," I said.

"Oh yeah, got it," he said.

About a week later, I met with the guys. They agreed to meet for about fifteen minutes every Wednesday before youth group to pray. After a year they were meeting regularly every Wednesday night to pray for each other. They did it all through high school. They became a serious influence on their high school by rising to significant leadership positions.

Remember: "Do not be misled: 'Bad company corrupts good character.'" But sometimes people use this verse to support the idea that we shouldn't hang out with nonChristian friends. That's not entirely what the verse means. It doesn't say we should avoid nonChristians. If we did that, we could never help them come to know Jesus as their Savior. It means that the strongest relationships we have must be with people who are a good influence.

So being a Christian in high school means choosing your friends wisely. It means more time to the good influencers than to the bad influencers. It means being the stronger good influence (even over little things) in the middle of the bad influence. Because you are letting God renew your mind.

5. *Always remember: It's the little things that affect the big things.* At the beginning of the chapter I told you that nobody wakes up and says, "I think I'll destroy my life today." The little compromises here and there start to become bigger and more consuming, until one day that person finds himself in a desperate state. Well, the opposite is true too.

The little things you do to honor God also impact the big things that honor God. When you make up your mind not to be influenced by the world around you, and to be influenced by God and His values, it becomes easier *not* to compromise.

There is more to Daniel's story in this regard. Daniel and his friends finally did graduate from governor's school, and so did many of the other students who were taken captive that day. They all were given positions as advisers and governors in Nebuchadnezzar's government. However, the four men stayed true to their commitment not to be influenced by the world. They were not going to bow to any pressure to conform to standards that God did not set.

This remained true all through their lives. But the commitment came with a price tag—some pain and suffering. Daniel was ultimately thrown into a roomful of hungry lions because he took that stand. He wasn't going to be squeezed by the influence of political leaders to alter his prayer life, even though they commanded him to stop praying for a while. Daniel decided to do what was right. And I'm convinced he would never have made it through something as big as the lion's den experience if he hadn't decided not to be influenced in the little things far ahead of time.

How about Hananiah, Azariah, and Mishael? These guys did the same. They faced the ultimate peer pressure—and I mean *heated* pressure. You might be familiar with their trial by fire. Their names were changed by Nebuchadnezzar to Shadrach, Meshach, and Abednego. They would face a fiery furnace in front of hundreds of thousands of dignitaries. They refused to bow to Nebuchadnezzar's golden idol and got thrown into the barbecue. You see, they had made up their mind that they would not bow to a bad influence.

Shadrach, Meshach, and Abednego took one of the most influential stands in all of Scripture. They told Nebuchadnezzar, "If we are thrown into the blazing furnace, the God we serve is able to save us from it, and he will rescue us from your hand, O king. But even if he does not, we want you to know, O king, that we will not serve your gods or worship the image of gold you have set up" (Daniel 3:17-18). These guys were not going to bow to the influence of the king, even if it meant losing their lives. It wasn't about the outcome. They said God *could* deliver them, but if He chose not to, they wanted to go on record: "We're not bowing."

These guys could never have done this unless they started with the little things. The foundation was laid for them way back in high school when they sat down to dinner. I imagine that these guys had a big poster in their room that said, "We Will *Not* Bow." They made up their minds, in high school, that they would be more influenced by the God who renews their mind than by a world that dulls it.

You want to be a Christian in high school? Think about this: Have you made up your mind that you will not bow to the influence of the world? Have you asked God to control your mind and transform it? Are you surrounding yourself with good and God-honoring influences?

Finally: When the pressure is on, will you bow? Because if you bow in the little things you will bow in the big things. Think about it.

If you want to be a Christian in high school, step around the moral land mines to avoid compromise at all costs.

THINK IT THROUGH

1. What is your reaction to the story of Daniel and his friends? What part of their story was most meaningful for you?

2. When are you most tempted to compromise? What makes it harder to resist? What makes it easier?

3. What are some of the areas in which popularity and doing the right thing have come into conflict in your life?

4. What little compromise could become a big problem for you?

5. How would you evaluate current friends' influence on how you make decisions? Overall, would you say your close friends are influencing good or bad decisions in your life? What are some examples?

6. Imagine losing a full scholarship to college because you decide to not compromise your belief about prayer or abortion in the application. How can this affect your future?

CHAPTER FOUR

JOSEPH: WOULD YOU GO FOR IT?

*He pushes open the kitchen door and walks into an empty room.
"Hey, where is everybody?" he yells.*

Then he sees her. The boss's wife. Waiting for . . . him.

*She's beautiful—and not wearing much. She grabs hold of
him, brings her lips up to his, starts to undress him. This is definitely getting hot.*

It's an average Tuesday night, and six high school guys walk to the
Caribou Coffee shop, where they've staked a claim to the corner table.
One by one they arrive, order their coffees, and head toward the back.
They've committed to meet every week to pray with each other, encour-
age each other, and hold each other accountable for spiritual growth.
Ron and Ryan are the last to arrive and, as they scoot into the booth,
Ron says, "It's hard to be a Christian with so many hot girls in the world."

The topic of the night: sex.

Ron echoed the frustrations of most high school students, guys and
girls alike. It is difficult to be Christian in high school and also have a
healthy, God-pleasing sexuality.

Clearly, as human beings, our spiritual nature and our sexual nature
are both gifts from God. Yet the "hormone factor" makes things so com-
plex. We know sex is good and has its rightful place in marriage. We
also know that lust is wrong and will lead us down destructive paths,

whether we're married or single. As writer Frederick Buechner once defined it: "Lust is the craving for salt of a person dying of thirst." The more we lust, the less satisfied we become.

Nevertheless, the teenage body is stuck in sexual overdrive (you've probably noticed that). And to complicate matters, the average teen receives so many different Christian messages about sex—

"You should be dating responsibly."
"Dating? You shouldn't be dating at all."
"Sex is good; it's a pleasurable gift from God."
"Sex was never meant for enjoyment—just for making babies."
"God wired you to have sexual drives and desires."
"You can overcome your sexual desires. Pray about it!"

That's just a sample of the long list of paired opposites flying around out there. I'm sure you could add some of your own, based on comments you've heard from parents, teachers, and youth pastors. Then mix in all the sexy advertisements, books, movies, and magazines the world bombards you with, and you can really set yourself up for living in defeat. So, exactly how *do* you stay Christian in high school and live as a sexual being?

Ron and Ryan knew they had to hold each other accountable for their spiritual growth. They were also developing personal disciplines for confronting the sexual stimuli swirling around them every day. "It seems like we're doing everything we can," Ron said. "So why is it still so tough not to act on temptations?"

"Well, just because you do everything humanly possible doesn't mean that God is going to eliminate the struggle," I said. "Remember, He wants us to continue to depend on Him in every situation. That includes the times when our desires call out to us to take the wrong actions."

"I understand that, but I think we have it harder than all those guys in Bible days," Ron replied. "They didn't have to deal with so much pressure."

"You don't think so?" I questioned. "Let's look at a young man in the Bible who fell into sexual sin. I want to see whether you can relate to him, even though we don't know his name."

THE GUY WITH JUMBLED JUDGMENT

I took the guys to the book of Proverbs, where Solomon, the wisest man who ever lived, tells a story about a young man who falls to lustful temptation. He implies many ideas that, if followed, will keep a person from sexual sin. The story comes through in Proverbs 7:6-23. (Suggestion: Take a moment to read this story in your Bible right now; keep your Bible open as we talk about it.)

Solomon tells us that one evening he's relaxing at home when he looks out the window and sees a young man who lacks judgment. The youth isn't stupid, but he could make a very stupid decision. How do we know this? Because he's walking back and forth in front of a hooker's house!

He knows she lives there, and he constantly takes the road leading past her house, constantly puts himself in a place where he can fall to sexual sin. He's always walking past the book rack where magazine-cover bikini girls shout: "Hey, big boy! Come spend some time with us. No one will know." He's always checking out certain websites on his computer, where "babe heaven" is just a click-of-the-mouse away. If he were smart, he wouldn't take that route. He wouldn't go to those stores, and he'd move his computer into his family's living room.

But Solomon says this guy is aimless, so he continues to walk by her house—deliberately, even at night—so that nobody sees him at a time when he knows he himself may see. May see some action.

After a while he gets what he wants. The woman just happens to be leaving the house, and—amazing!—he's standing right there. But did he really know what he was getting himself into? The sights and sounds and ideas—she's a real smooth talker—rush at him, throwing him into psychic overload . . .

> *My hubby's not home . . . come on, it won't be a problem . . . give me a kiss . . . and she's HOT. . . . I've got some new sheets . . . and smell this perfume? . . . no, he won't be home for weeks, so who cares . . . give me a kiss, I said . . . come on in, sit down . . . how about a drink? . . . look at those legs . . . let me take your coat . . .*

Who's doing the talking, and who's listening? It's hard to tell when you're suddenly in the grip of temptation. This young man with no judgment becomes jumbled. Solomon looks at this and says it's truly a dangerous situation. He compares this poor guy to an ox about to be slaughtered.

Now, an ox is a stupid animal. If an ox is slated for butchering, it will inevitably happen because that ox doesn't have a brain to discern the danger. It doesn't read the sign on the side of the building that reads "Joe's Meat Market." It doesn't devise a plan that includes a *Matrix*-style kung fu fight and an escape route.

Nope. That ox just follows the rear of the ox in front of it . . . without thinking . . . until the lights go out. The point is, you're *not* a dumb ox, so *think*. You do have the capability to see the issues and to discern truth, to know right and wrong. The Holy Spirit does stir within you to motivate you to get out of those situations. Can you do it?

Another teen in the Bible faced the same type of Hey-Big-Boy sexual temptation. Would he go for it?

Would *you*? If you could just have sex without all the complications? Hard to imagine, but it happened to one of the nicest kids you'd ever want to meet. Somebody just like . . . you.

THE STAGE IS SET

Joseph was number eleven of twelve sons. He was the favorite of his father, Jacob, and Joseph's brothers had a difficult time with this. They were jealous, resenting the favoritism.

Joseph didn't help matters. He would have dreams in which all his brothers were bowing down to him. Now, if you're the younger brother with ten that are older than you, and you already know they despise you, is it wise to tell them they're going to bow down to you? (Even if the dreams did come from God.)

After Joseph reveals his dreams, the brothers decide they've had it with little brother. They want to get rid of him, so they begin to plot. They'll kill Joseph and make it look like an accident.

One day, when they're out of town doing business, Jacob sends Joseph to check up on them. When they see Joseph coming, they decide to carry out their plan. Fortunately for Joseph, one of the elder brothers has a moment of compassion and persuades the others to spare the lad. This brother, Reuben, wants to get Joseph back home, ASAP. But before he can send Joseph away, the other brothers sell him as a slave to an Egyptian merchant who's passing by. What a great plan! They can get the little creep out of their hair and make a good chunk of pocket change too.

So Joseph is soon riding a camel headed for the Nile. When he arrives in Egypt, he's sold again to Potiphar, an influential and powerful man in Pharaoh's government, probably chief adviser to this Egyptian king.

RISING THROUGH THE RANKS

Joseph is only seventeen years old as all of these things take place. Yet the Bible says he continuously trusted in the Lord. He was passionate about pleasing God. As a result, God blesses him and gives him success as he works for Potiphar. In fact, Scripture says that everything Joseph did prospered.

Of course, this made Potiphar very happy, and he took an incredible liking to Joseph. He continued to give Joseph more and more responsibilities, more and more control over his own household—until Joseph was running the whole show for Potiphar.

Imagine it. This teenager is so successful that he's handling the affairs of one of the leading heads of state in Egypt. The only thing Potiphar concerned himself with was the dinner menu. He didn't want to hear about problems with his household staff; Joseph took care of it. He didn't need to see any of the bills; Joseph paid them. He didn't even have to worry about his weekly appointments; Joseph managed the day planner.

Potiphar just wanted to come home and say, "Hey, what's for dinner?" And he expected an immediate answer. There was nothing Joseph didn't control in Potiphar's home and business affairs.

So the Bible talks about Joseph's success in Potiphar's household. But then there's a turn in the plot. In the middle of a particular verse, we find a seemingly out-of-place statement. Read Genesis 39:6: "So [Potiphar] left everything that he owned in Joseph's charge; and with him there he did not concern himself with anything except the food which he ate. Now Joseph was handsome in form and appearance" (NASB).

Did you catch it? What do Joseph's *looks* have to do with anything? Yet God wanted us to know that Joseph was a stud. He was very good looking and, as a matter of fact, was probably supermodel material. Everyone was impressed by Joseph's great build and handsome looks . . . especially Potiphar's wife.

Every day that Potiphar's wife sees Joseph, she becomes more and more attracted to him. Soon she wants Joseph bad. She starts to make advances, but Joseph just shrugs them off. She offers sexually overt compliments, but Joseph just smiles and gets a little embarrassed. Soon it becomes apparent that her advances aren't working, so she gets more aggressive and more obvious. Eventually, she comes right out with it: "Let's go to bed, Joseph."

She's not even hinting. Joseph has an open invitation. That's sexual pressure!

I was telling Ron and Ryan this story, and one of them said, "Yuck, an old married woman making a pass at a seventeen year old! *That* wouldn't be hard to resist." Well, if you think Potiphar's wife was like your mom, then maybe it wouldn't be tempting. But knowing the Egyptian customs might change your mind.

You see, the Egyptians believed in an afterlife. They believed that when a person died, especially a significant person like Pharaoh or Potiphar, then that person could take prize possessions—and sometimes even people—along with him to "the other side." Because they always wanted to be ready for death, the officials who were close to Pharaoh would frequently take on new and younger wives. This often involved an elaborate beauty pageant in which women from all over the land could come with hopes of being selected. Needless to say, Potiphar's wife was *not* an old hag. She was probably a young, hot, recent beauty-pageant winner. Doesn't that make a big difference in understanding the temptation here? Joseph faces a babe, not a hag.

She'd often find Joseph and attempt to carry out her sexual plan. "We'll be the only ones to know, Joseph," she would say. "Come on! My husband is at work all day."

They could have great sex during the day and, since Potiphar was only concerned about the dinner menu, he'd never catch on. Think of the affection she'd lavish on Joseph. And she'd probably appeal to his ego by telling him he was the best looking guy in all of Egypt.

So Joseph has a hot beauty queen, openly inviting him, *every day* to have wild, passionate sex. Wow! Now that's incredible sexual pressure. The guys quickly agreed that it was more sexual pressure than they ever faced.

THINGS HEAT UP

Each time she attempts to seduce Joseph, he shuts her down. He reminds her that Potiphar hasn't withheld anything that he owns from Joseph—except his wife. "How can I do this great evil and sin against God?" asks Joseph.

That's interesting. Joseph says Potiphar has given him all these great things, but the sin would be against . . . *God!* Joseph was connected to God. His perspective was God-honoring.

Potiphar's wife isn't seeing things the same way. She's determined to break Joseph down and get what she wants, so she devises a plan to make this already sexually hot situation even hotter. First, she gives all the servants a day off. Normally Joseph would know about this, because he's in charge. But she makes sure nobody reveals her plan. Next, with all the servants out of the house, she can turn up the heat even more; maybe Joseph will finally drop his guard.

Imagine it. Joseph gets up one morning. He prepares for work and starts to go through his daily routine. He walks out to the mailbox to get the daily mail and newspaper. He comes into the house and walks across the foyer of his master's mansion. He's checking out the mail as he makes his way to the kitchen.

But something's very peculiar. The place seems awfully quiet. He looks to the left into the dining room, where the maid is usually polishing silverware. But she isn't there today. *That's odd,* he thinks. He looks to the right into the living room. Usually the butler is there at the desk organizing the day's affairs, but he's not there today either. Joseph goes to the window and notices that the gardener and chauffeur aren't around. *Maybe they're all in the kitchen with the cook?* Joseph pushes open the kitchen door to find that the kitchen is empty, and the cook, with all his staff, is gone.

"Hey, where is everybody?" he yells. "I think you all need to get back to work!"

He continues to call as he retraces his steps back to the foyer. When he arrives at the base of the stairs, he sees her. Potiphar's wife is there waiting for him. She is beautiful, and she is determined to have him. She isn't wearing very much either. He has never seen so much of her before and, while the situation is uncomfortable, he finds his blood pressure rising.

She grabs hold of him and starts putting moves on him. Joseph realizes this is going to be the most difficult test yet. He's feeling the sexual pressure greater than ever before.

She starts to kiss him.

Joseph hesitates.

She starts to undress him. This is getting unbearably hot, and Joseph knows he needs to get out of there. He knows that if he doesn't act on God's prompting immediately, he will end up rationalizing things. She already has much of his clothes in her hands!

Without explanation Joseph bolts out of there. He doesn't worry about whether he's going to hurt her feelings. He doesn't stay to enjoy some of it and then draw the line when it starts to go too far. He doesn't rationalize about how strong he is. He just *runs!*

WHERE DO WE GO FROM HERE?

Deep in your heart you know Joseph's crisis is little different from the kinds of sexual decisions you face regularly as a Christian high schooler. Lust is always calling, whether you live in ancient Egypt or modern-day Homeville.

But perhaps you were expecting some set-in-stone formula for dealing with sexual temptation? Sorry, it's just not that easy. First of all, let's all admit: High school students are at a developmental stage in life at which they must formulate their own values about the big life issues. One of those value-loaded issues is sexuality. God's Word talks about it and provides many guidelines—everything from how to have sexual conversations to enjoying sexual intercourse.

Why is this the case? It's because God created sex, and He made it good. He designed it for procreation *and* for our pleasure. *He is all about sex!* (I said that to a group of seventh-graders once, and a little quiet kid sitting in the front row said, *"Sweet!"*). God *is* all about sex, and that *is* sweet. As a matter of fact, an entire book of the Bible, the Song of Solomon, waxes eloquent on the topic of sexual pleasure. (When I tell high school students that, I am amazed at how many commit to starting personal Bible study . . . in *that* book!)

When you start formulating Christian values about sexuality, realize that the Bible—as with many other life areas—often gives us *principles* (like remaining sexually pure) without certain *specifics*. In other words, Scripture isn't always black and white about sexuality, and sometimes the vagueness creates a gray zone or gives rise to what I'd call a "wisdom issue."

A wisdom issue is a topic that Scripture doesn't speak to directly or comprehensively. It is an issue that may create tension because godly people can line up on either side of questions about "where to draw the line," or exactly what is okay or not okay. For example, is masturbation okay? What about oral sex in marriage? Or contraception? Bible believing Christians disagree about such things. Therefore, I believe God deliberately designed wisdom issues for at least three reasons:

1. *Wisdom issues make us run to God.* God created us for fellowship with Himself. He wants us to trust in Him. However, we've become people who trust in our own ideas about things, so God throws in a few wisdom

issues to make us constantly run back to Him. In such situations, the standard we seek may not be as concrete as we desire. That means that an action may be sin for one person but not for another. So . . . I must be incredibly sensitive to the Holy Spirit's leading and must constantly run to God with this issue. (Please pause here to read Romans 14, which offers a glimpse into an ancient wisdom issue and how Paul advised believers to deal with it.)

2. *Wisdom issues make Scripture timeless.* The Bible is the rule and authority for the Christian life. It is the Word of God. Therefore, it's timeless while the culture around us is not. Things change. Old ideas fade away and new ideas surface. At times the Bible doesn't speak directly to certain issues because it is not locked into a specific cultural time frame. Wisdom issues allow us to apply biblical principles that guide us amid changing times.

3. *Wisdom issues demonstrate Christian liberty—and bondage to Christ.* Naturally, I must avoid certain things in order to keep my relationship with Christ growing. That doesn't mean all of my Christian brothers and sisters must avoid the same things (remember Romans 14). Facing a wisdom issue will make me exercise disciplines that keep me growing in my relationship with God. For example, for Big Bob eating dessert may be sin, because he struggles with gluttony. It may be perfectly fine for Skinny Minny though. There is liberty and there is restraint in the Christian life. A wisdom issue creates that tension and definition.

I'm saying all this to let you know up front that you may not find all the answers set in stone when it comes to determining what you may or may not do in a relationship—or in answering questions like, "How far is too far?" But you *will* find that the Bible is extremely important in helping you formulate your values about sexuality. If you listen closely to God's Word you'll better understand many of the mixed messages hurtling toward you every day.

So seek the Lord about these things. Be sincere about doing the right thing. Ask God to guard and renew your mind. Then understand that usually the people who offer so many of those conflicting messages are God-honoring men and women. But they've come to different conclusions. God is going to direct *you* to conclusions, as well.

Having nailed down the concept of wisdom issues, there are a couple more things to know about sexuality. I've got two more ideas for you to consider, as you make your own decisions amid your future go-for-it temptations:

Sexual thinking and lust—it's all about total surrender. Is every sexual thought or desire lust? Nope. God created you sexual. And that is a very good thing. We've already seen that He made you so that you would have sexual desires, and He made those sexual desires unique to you. Therefore, just because something sexually excites you doesn't mean it's lustful.

Some teens respond by adding: "But if you dwell on that, then you're lusting." The question then is: How much "think time" about a sexual thing is too much "think time"? The answer surely has to do with balance.

The Bible teaches us about having a balanced and controlled life. We're not to be mastered by anything: "'Everything is permissible for me'—but I will not be mastered by anything" (1 Corinthians 6:12). You can think about sex, and think about it a lot, as long as it doesn't master you. There is no "amount" put on it. And the control part is simply this: *Don't let anything control you but God.* Totally surrender your life and mind to Him.

Easy arousal—it's all about the daily menu. Feeling guilty about being so easily sexually aroused? Eric, for example, came into my office looking down at the floor as if he'd lost a contact lens in my nice, plush car-peting. "I've asked God to control my sexual thoughts," he said. "But He never does it."

Eric told me he tried not to overload his life with sexual stimuli. This is important. You can't ask God to control you, and then consume a steady intake of sexually charged movies, music, computer games, and magazines. But as hard as Eric tried, he was still always so "horny" (as he put it).

"God has turned on a steady stream of hormones in your body, Eric," I said. "These hormones are essential for your physical develop-ment. They are also responsible for making you sexually aroused. To pray that God will stop that? Not going to happen. Your hormone surge is keeping you healthy."

So is there something you can do to get some of it under control? Yes! You can realize that those hormones are like an appetite. Having an appetite is natural and inevitable. But the more you feed it, the more ferocious it can become. What will you feed it today? What's on the daily menu of your imagination? If you want to stay Christian in high school, then monitor your imagination menu.

Think about it!

If you want to stay Christian in high school, constantly monitor your Mind-Menu — and leave temporary pleasures behind.

THINK IT THROUGH

1. Have you ever faced a go-for-it sexual situation? How did you deal with it?

2. What advice would you give a friend who keeps falling to this type of temptation? What portions of Scripture might help you?

3. Which truths or principles in this chapter help you the most with your own sexual struggles? Why?

4. In your opinion, what made the difference between Joseph and the guy in Proverbs — causing them to make such different choices?

5. Think ahead for a moment: What is the next tempting situation you are likely to face? How are you preparing yourself for this event?

CHAPTER FIVE

JAMES AND JOHN: PARTY HEARTY

"Mine went farther!"

"Yeah, right! Are you blind? I threw it miles ahead of your rock!"

"Keep dreaming, John. You throw like a girl. I'm surprised you could even pick up that rock, you're so weak and girly."

"Shut up, puss-arm."

"You ought to talk, sissy."

"Let's ask Bartholomew. Hey, Bartholomew!" . . .

Jesus called them the Sons of Thunder. But why? Maybe James and John were teenage party animals? They might have referred to themselves as "Rock" and "Roll," a *thunderous* party waiting to happen. Or maybe it was because they were constantly "exploding" in anger. That would have made one Nitro and the other Glycerin. Or maybe it was because of their constant competitive spirit. Thunder crashed when brother "push" met brother "shove." At any rate they got the tag "Sons of Thunder" from Jesus. Some Bible historians believe that James was about sixteen years old and John, his brother, was about fourteen when Jesus invited them to be His disciples. Imagine, Jesus chooses the Sons of Thunder to be apostles. Picture this . . .

The first time these two meet Jesus, they're sitting on the dock mending Dad's fishing nets. They have to help their dad because the night before they'd been out late with friends. It was the last day of school, and everybody was amped.

What do you do to kick off summer break? Go to a movie? No. There had to be something more exciting. "Let's go over to my house," says one of the guys. "My parents are in Egypt for the weekend. The whole place is ours."

Party! James starts to put out the word, and soon half the school is planning to be there. John knows that one of his friend's older brothers can buy beer, so he calls and gets it all set up. *This is going to be one great bash.*

The party starts out mild, though—friends sitting around talking, listening to music, playing Xbox—just hanging out. Soon the beer arrives, and more and more people. James and his brother, John, are the life of the party.

As the evening progresses, James' friends tell him that a few of the girls really like him and John. "You should go talk to them," says one guy. James is smooth, so he goes over and starts the conversation. As he talks, one of the girls asks about John. With that, James calls John into the conversation. *What could be better?* they think. *All this attention from two beautiful young ladies. . . .* Just then a whole new group of friends bursts through the front door.

One of the newcomers wants to "show them something" in the backyard. In a dark corner of the patio, he opens a bag of "recreational drugs." The Sons of Thunder have smoked pot before, so they were pretty stoked to see the buffet of goodies this guy had snuck in. "Let's get a little buzzed," John says, "before rejoining the ladies."

The girls come out to see what's going on, and they decide to join the fun. Thunder Boys think the whole situation is sweet. The conversation is cool, the friends are great, the buzz is outrageous. And soon things start to get romantic. The group starts to couple up as the conversation becomes more sexually charged. It won't be long before everybody's looking for a little privacy.

Mom wasn't too happy when James and John arrived the next morning still a little wasted. She told them to sleep it off in their rooms and wait until their father got home.

They both feel like garbage as they walk to their rooms. They also feel worse thinking of the coming judgment of their father. "Why do we do those stupid things?" James says to John.

"Because it's fun, and besides, our friends do it too so it's not like we're doing anything wrong," John says. "It's just part of growing up, average teenager stuff; it's just being part of the gang."

That night when Mr. Zebedee (their father) arrived home, it didn't take long for Mom and Dad to be in conference over the events of the previous evening. James and John tried to hear what they were privately talking about in the other room, but couldn't make anything out. They were talking too quietly.

Dinner was tense. There was hardly a word said. James and John just looked at their plates as they ate. They didn't want to bring on any wrath before it's time. Occasionally each brother would catch the eye of the other across the table. They both kept giving each other the "this-is-all-your-fault" look. Finally, Dad broke the silence.

"Your mother and I have had a long talk about you two. Coming in at all hours of the night after partying with friends is just not acceptable," he said quietly. "Beginning tomorrow morning and every day for the rest of the summer, you are both going to work for me. I'll expect to see you awake, dressed, and ready to go at 5 A.M. You boys are going to be painting and cleaning the boats. Maybe if you guys have to work all day, you'll think twice about staying out all night." With that the conversation was over. Both boys felt as if they had been doomed to a fate worse than death.

The sun was so hot on the Galilee shores and the docks smelled so foul. Visions came to mind: scrubbing the decks of those smelly boats with all the fish guts all over them or hanging on the side of the boat painting in the sweltering sun. They knew that they would come home absolutely exhausted each night. If they had to get up at 5 A.M. every day they would be in bed really early each night out of exhaustion, which also meant no social life! And then there was their boss, *Dad*, the worst taskmaster of all. He would be on them all the time, never letting them slow down and always inspecting their work until it was done to perfection.

Both guys just sat there in a daze. *This is going to be the summer from hell*, James thought. It is at this point in their lives that they meet a man named Jesus.

Jesus began to teach and heal people throughout the region where James and John lived. People all over were talking about the amazing things this prophet-teacher was doing. Stories were circulating all over the docks and James and John were fascinated.

One day Jesus was down by the docks. A small group of people had gathered around Him. James and John were sitting on the dock next to the boat mending the broken nets. They hated this job most of all because it was like untying a huge knot, only this knot was wet, stinky, and had fish parts all over it. They could see the group getting larger and they wanted to go over there to see the commotion. Zeb had just come on deck because he too heard the crowd. He was standing over the place where James and John were working.

"Dad, can we take a break and go over there to hear what Jesus is saying?" John asked.

"No, you boys need to finish the job," Zeb replied as he looked over the side of the boat, down at the boys who were sitting on the dock in the middle of all the fishing nets, sweating in the hot sun.

"We won't take long, Dad; just let us go for a few minutes," James piped in.

"I said no. Keep mending," he said sternly and without hesitation.

Just then the crowd started to move toward their direction. All three Zebedee men watched as Jesus came walking down the dock near their boat. When Jesus saw James and John He stopped and said, "Hey guys, come and follow me, and I'll make you real fishers of men."

When Jesus looks at the Sons of Thunder, He sees two young men in need of some major overhauling. They're going to follow their dad and be fishermen, of course. . . . But there is something about Jesus. Is it the look of total confidence beaming from his face? Or perhaps it's the inviting smile, tinged with a flicker of humor?

James and John looked up from their perch at the stern figure of their father standing over them on the bow of the boat. He looked down at his boys with that stone-cold emotionless, firm, concentration camp commander look and said, "Go ahead, get out of here!"

With almost reflex-like reaction both boys jumped up, grabbed the nets, and threw them onto the deck of the boat. "Thanks, Dad," James shouted. "Yeah, you're the best, Dad," John added, as they ran down the dock to catch up with Jesus.

Little did they know that everything was about to change.

CAN YOU RELATE?

Just like you, James and John became followers of Jesus when they were teenagers. Catch this, Jesus chose teenagers to be a part of the Twelve that He would call apostles. Average teenagers! Just like you, James and John had to learn how to stay Christian in high school. From the story you can see that these guys didn't have it all together, nor did they get it all together immediately after they followed Jesus. It was going to take some work.

FIGHTING AND COMPETING, AGAIN AND AGAIN

Fast-forward to a small band of disciples following Jesus through the countryside. The group now includes the Sons of Thunder.

It was hardly a secret that James and John constantly competed. They bickered all the time, driving the other disciples crazy. Everything was a contest between these two. As they walked the dirt paths from village to village with Jesus, they'd invent games to pass the time. James would pick up a rock and challenge John to see who could throw it farthest. If it became a close call, they would start fighting.

"Mine went farther," James would declare.

"Yeah, *right*! Are you blind? I threw it miles ahead of your rock!" John would reply.

"Keep dreamin'; you throw like a girl. I'm surprised you could even pick up that rock, you're so weak and girly."

"Shut up, puss-arm."

"You ought to talk, sissy."

"Let's ask Bartholomew. Hey, *Bartholomew!*"

The other ten disciples are ready to kill these two kids. Bartholomew rolls his eyes. *What was Jesus thinking when He picked these two guys?* The competing, the challenging, the never-ending rivalry!

And they hardly thought about anyone but themselves. They didn't care that they were driving the other disciples nuts. They didn't mind embarrassing them in every city and village they entered. They certainly didn't realize that the desire always to be first showed everyone their true colors: extreme self-centeredness, selfish to the max.

All James could think about was James, and all John could think about was John. How could anyone who was following Jesus day by day be so self-absorbed? The competitive spirit became so consuming that it created thunderous explosions at every turn.

But think: Can you stay Christian in high school that way? Or must you let go of a competitive, fighting, arguing spirit? Could Nitro and Glycerin let go?

Talk about self-centered! James and John were so competitive that they even fought about who was better at following Jesus. The boys worried about coming out on top. They refused to see themselves as loser material. These guys were so self-centered they even treated their selfishness as if it were a spiritual virtue. Here's what I mean: One day Jesus was talking about the kingdom of God, as usual. Later, walking along, James and John made their own personal applications.

"I can't wait," says John. "I want to have a big house in that kingdom."

"I want a mansion," James says.

"Well, Jesus likes me a lot, so I think He's going to give me plenty of servants too."

"He might like you, but He thinks I'm really cool. He'll probably let me be a mayor in one of the kingdom cities, kind of like how Joseph ruled in Egypt."

"Well, if He gives you a city, He'll give me a bigger one."

"You're always thinking about yourself, John. Did you ever stop to think that maybe Jesus might let me rule next to Him?"

"Next to Him?" John questioned. "What do you mean? Like you think you'll have a throne next to Jesus? You're so dumb!"

James stops his brother John dead in the road and looks him sternly in the eye. Without even blinking and in all seriousness, he says, "Joseph ruled in Egypt, Daniel ruled in Babylon, and I'm no different from them."

Now John is thinking his brother may have a point. "I'm going to rule with Him too!"

"You are not. *Two* people can't rule with Him."

"Sure can," John replies. "I'll be His right-hand man and you can be . . . *umm* . . . His left-hand man."

"Wrong, bucko. I'll be the right, and you'll be the left."

"You don't even know your left from your right!" And the fight begins, a series of verbal punches followed by a couple takedown attempts.

"Okay! Let's ask Jesus!"

The Sons of Thunder go to Jesus and ask whether they can rule with Him, one on His left and the other on His right (read about it in Mark 10:35-45). They are so self-absorbed that they don't even realize the other disciples are listening to the whole thing.

Jesus asks James and John whether they're able to drink the cup that He would drink and experience the baptism He'd have to endure. He was talking about the suffering to come. Naturally, they tell Jesus, "Of course we can!"

As the other disciples become more indignant, Jesus gathers them all for a teaching session. He tells His followers that the cup He would drink and the baptism He would experience meant more than just suffering humiliation. It included *serving* in humility. Jesus tells them that to be great they must be the servant of the rest. And if they want to be first they must see themselves as last. As the least. As the slave of the rest.

He was always saying such things . . .

The last will be first.
It's better to give than to receive.
Treat others better than you treat yourself.
Lose your life to find it.
Die if you want to live.

Being a disciple yourself, how do you apply those words of Jesus? If you want to stay Christian in high school you have to give Jesus control over your selfish ambitions and let Him develop a servant's heart in you.

///

Not long ago I met a girl named Julie, a sophomore in high school. She'd just returned from a mission trip to Haiti with her youth group. "I didn't realize how selfish and self-absorbed I was," she told me, "until I saw these little kids who had nothing, and yet they were so happy." When Julie came home, she felt nauseated and ashamed of all the stuff that she had—and how much she expected others to serve her. "I had never thought about *really* serving others."

I asked her what she meant.

"Well, I guess I've only so-called 'served' others when I had to, like when my youth group did outreach projects."

So guess what happened? Julie started to pray *that God would give her a servant's heart.* She was convicted by all the stuff she had, so she started giving things away. She also began to look for projects she could do on her own. She found opportunities to commit random acts of kindness. She went to nursing homes and read books to the elderly. She arranged to babysit free, for moms with little kids so they could have a break once in a while.

Julie became a servant with a servant's heart. If you want to stay Christian in high school, you have to follow Christ, the one who "did not come to be served, but to serve, and to give his life as a ransom for many" (Mark 10:45).

Unlike James and John, Julie demonstrates that if you want to stay Christian in high school, you'll need to give Jesus control over your competitive spirit and self-centered ambitions. Let Him develop a servant's heart in you.

INSENSITIVE AND HURTFUL

Back to James and John. Besides the fighting and self-centeredness, I think Jesus saw something else in these teens that made him call them Sons of Thunder. I think they were arrogant hotheads. My guess is that they said things and did things that were very hurtful to others. Without thinking, they probably struck quickly and electrocuted innocent bystanders just as a shot of lightning would.

They were always butting heads with each other and constantly in rivalry over everything. Their argumentative and hot-tempered spirits were a constant exhaustion to their friends and family.

One day they were at each other's throats. James started to aggravate John, and John decided that he had had about all he could take. They started to throw insults at each other. That began a war of words. As the war of words started to rise, so did the levels of their voices. They didn't realize that they were yelling at each other. Their mom was at the other end of the house and she could hear every word. She was starting to lose her patience because this was becoming a regular event in their home.

James started in on John, telling him that he was a "wuss" because of some stupid thing that John said. John retaliated by calling James a few choice names while throwing an elbow to his stomach as he walked past him. James struck back by pushing John and the roughhousing began.

Mom was just about at the end of her rope. She picked up her broom (that was Mom's teenage-boy-tool-of-discipline) and made her way toward the now existing battle zone. It sounded like they were killing each other. Mom was furious. She could hear them upstairs in the hall banging into the walls, throwing each other on the floor, pushing each other around, all the while yelling and screaming at each other. The mild altercation had become the testosterone-fueled hurricane that barreled through their home almost daily now. She held her broom in hand like she was holding a rifle with a blazing bayonet. "I've had it with those two! Those boys are about to meet my broom," she muttered under her breath. When she got to the top of the stairs she saw the two of them on top of each other rolling on the floor. They were each intertwined with the other so that it was hard to tell which body part was James' and which was John's, yet each had managed to get an arm free, and they were frantically throwing punches and flailing away at what they thought was the other guy's torso.

Mom attacked the hurricane using the broomstick to pry John off of James' back. She managed to position herself between the two so they would settle down. "I don't know what to do with you boys!" she shouted. "This is going to stop. I'm sick and tired of this fighting and competition between the two of you. I've had about all I can take. This has got to stop once and for all," she said as she tried to catch her breath, exhausted from her conquest with the J & J storm.

Sibling rivalry was just one way that their tempers flared. I imagine that, since these guys couldn't control their tempers in their own home, it probably came out in public too. They always had the safety off and their finger on the trigger ready to fire at the littlest thing.

James and John are having one of their days—arguing, fighting. They stop for lunch at McDavid's, "the king of all burgers" place, and of course, they're rude to the staff. The anger that rages in them starts to come out in sarcastic remarks. They pick up an abandoned newspaper and start reading about a guy who got beat up and robbed by some Samaritan thugs.

James and John can't stand the Samaritans. As a matter of fact, most of the Jews can't stand the Samaritans. "If anyone ever tried to rob me," says James, "I'd beat the living daylights out of him."

"Hey, I'd kill the guy," says John. "It would be self-defense, right?"

They continue to talk, fantasizing about organizing a group to go out, find the robbers, and kick their Samaritan butts. They leave the restaurant and, just as they get outside, a man approaches Jesus with a question: "What must I do to have eternal life?"

The two teens have heard Jesus answer questions like this before. But this time Jesus gets their attention. Jesus tells the man that he should love God with all his heart, soul, strength, and mind, and that he should love his neighbor as himself. The man doesn't seem to get the point, so he asks Jesus, "But who is my neighbor?"

In response, Jesus tells a story: "A man was going down from Jerusalem to Jericho, when he fell into the hands of robbers. They stripped him of his clothes, beat him and went away, leaving him half dead" (Luke 10:30).

Jesus sees that the Sons of Thunder are beginning to get ticked off. They're ready for Jesus to give the order, and they'll grab their weapons to kick some robber butt. Before Nitro and Glycerin can explode, though, Jesus throws a "now it just so happened that . . ." into His story. Immediately Thunder Boys are engaged again, because there is more to the story. "A priest happened to be going down the same road, and when he saw the man, he passed by on the other side. So too, a Levite, when he came to the place and saw him, passed by on the other side. But a Samaritan, as he traveled, came where the man was" (verses 31-33).

That Samaritan lowlife, James thinks. He'll probably steal anything else the poor guy has.

John's mind is churning too: If that punk touches the guy . . .

But the Samaritan stops and has compassion for the beaten man! He risks his own life by taking time in that canyon to bandage up the man's wounds. Then the Samaritan puts the man on his donkey. He knows that this is going to slow down his own journey, because now he has to walk miles. The compassionate Samaritan will get this guy to safety, no matter what.

James looks at John. "Compassionate Samaritan?" *Why would such a lowlife want to help?*

Jesus knows what these guys are thinking. He tells how the Samaritan travels miles with the wounded man. He stops frequently to tend to the poor guy's wounds. If he hadn't done that, the man surely would have died.

They continue on until they get to a village. Once there, the Samaritan takes the wounded man to a shelter where he can receive medical care and be nurtured back to health. The Samaritan was told that the man's recovery would take a long time, and that it would be costly—about $800 a day.

James and John look at each other with bulging eyes. "Whoa, eight hundred bucks a day?"

Jesus repeats it and continues to tell how the Samaritan runs down to the nearest ATM machine, withdraws $1,600, and gives it to the shelter director. The Samaritan tells the director he'll be back in two days with more money. He will pay whatever it takes to get this man back to health. The man's life was saved because of that compassionate Samaritan.

Now, about that original neighbor question, listen to the Scripture:

> *"Which of these three do you think was a neighbor to the man who fell into the hands of robbers?"*
>
> *The expert in the law replied, "The one who had mercy on him."*
>
> *Jesus told him, "Go and do likewise." (Luke 10:36-37)*

James and John are probably silent at this point. How would they feel? They look back on the past hour, see themselves being rude to the workers in McD's, and then wanting to rage on some people thought to be Samaritans. And now they see this guy in Jesus' story being more loving and sacrificing than they'd ever think of being. How would you feel?

III

Here is where the Sons of Thunder really start to change. You see, their hearts were melted by the love of Jesus. By His words, by His presence, by His example, by His prayers for them. They began to realize that *they couldn't really love God if they didn't love others.*

Can you relate? Can you love the unlovable?

Careful how you answer! It will knock you down a few notches on the cool scale if you talk to the person nobody cares for. It might make some people avoid you, if you don't join them in poking fun at the "loser." Some kids may reject you. But if you want to stay Christian in high school, then you're going to have to be all about . . . *love*.

I think about David, a senior, active in all kinds of leadership positions at school. He used to worry about what people thought of him, until summer camp between his sophomore and junior years. When he went back to school, he decided to stop trying to blend in. It was going to be okay to stand out as a Christian. And it would be okay to be more loving.

God put David to the test that year. He was president of the student body and had often spoken in front of the entire school. One day, Ryan, a skinny little freshman, came up to him and said: "I want to hang out with you and be your friend."

David agreed, even though he knew his popular friends would never hang with this guy. However, Ryan kept hanging; David kept being kind. Often Dave had to pray for love, because it started to get a bit irritating.

Finally, the big test: David was eating lunch in the cafeteria. Ryan came and sat with David, alongside many of David's "cool" friends. Those friends were seriously annoyed, and some took it upon themselves to ridicule the poor freshman.

What did David do? Did he trash Ryan too? Did he ditch his new friend and make excuses for why he had to leave him behind? No. He stood up to his arrogant friends and defended Ryan. One of Dave's friends blurted, "I don't know why you tolerate that kid; he's so freakin' *weird!*" And with that, they all walked away, leaving David and Ryan at the table alone.

"Don't pay attention to them, Ryan," Dave said. "They sometimes don't think before they speak." Then the two sat silently for a few seconds (but it seemed like an hour) before Ryan finally broke the silence. He said he used to believe in Jesus, but in junior high he decided that Christianity was a bunch of lies. Why? Because his family was really hurt bad by some people who said they were Christians. Ryan decided he wouldn't ever believe in Jesus; he'd be an atheist instead. "But over the past few weeks you have been so cool to me," he said. "And for the first time in my life, I've actually seen Jesus. If you are like Jesus, then I want to be a Christian like you."

If you want to stay Christian in high school, then love, love, love, with a servant's heart. Pray to love the unlovable.

SONS WITH SERVANT HEARTS

Remember the first scene when Jesus called the guys to follow Him? That was the beginning of a gradual, heart-deep change in James and John. I know Jesus' call changed these guys because later in his life, John will write more about love in his gospel (and in the epistles of First, Second, and Third John) than any other New Testament writer.

When John writes the gospel of John, he reminds us that Jesus says His disciples are marked by one key character quality: love. Jesus said, "A new commandment I give to you, that you love one another, even as I have loved you, that you also love one another. By this all men will know that you are My disciples, if you have love for one another" (John 13:34-35, NASB). The number one distinctive that separates Christians from everyone else is not how godly they are. It's not how much truth they know. It's not even how good they are. *It's how much they love.*

Over and over, John tells us to love. He says:

- God so loved the world that He gave His only Son (John 3:16).

- The love of the Father is in us (John 14:21).

- We love God by keeping His commandments (John 14:23-24).

- The Father and the Son love us (John 15:9).

- We can abide in love (John 15:10).

- There is no greater love than laying down your life for a friend (John 15:13).

- People will see Christ in us when we love (John 17:26).

- The love of God becomes perfect in us (1 John 2:5).

- God pours His love on us and calls us His children (1 John 3:1).

- We know love because Christ laid down His life for us (1 John 3:16).

- When we are loving, we show that we know God (1 John 4:7-17).

- Love casts out fear (1 John 4:18).

Love is the distinguishing mark on the life of a Jesus disciple. It makes us sons (children) of God. Imagine that! James and John went from being Sons of Thunder to sons of God. They were transformed by love.

If you want to stay Christian in high school, then soak in God's love for you and let it flow out to others. Start by praying that Jesus will make you awesomely aware of how beloved you are in His sight. Also, if you want to stay Christian in high school, love God with all your heart, soul, strength, and mind, and the loving others will start to happen.

Invite Him to make you a loving person, just as He is loving. If you do this, you'll face some tough decisions.

USING THE REPLACEMENT PRINCIPLE IN YOUR LIFE

I believe that over time James and John had to rethink the company they kept. They had to let go of certain "fun" activities. (I bet it was hard to say they weren't going to party anymore.) They had to give over to the Lord certain habits of thought and speech that made them fight, compete, and trash-talk. They probably had to give up hanging out with some friends that were into the party scene. They had to break old habits that they formed by avoiding certain places and influences. They had to get close to Jesus, and they found He operated on something I call the *Replacement Principle*.

The Replacement Principle works like this: If you want something out of your life, don't work hard to remove it. Instead, pour in something else that pushes it out. Replace something bad with something godly. To stay Christian in high school, *replace rotten stuff in your life with good stuff.*

John writes about this too. I think he learned the lesson well when he was a teenager. In 1 John he tells you that God desires to make your joy full and complete (1:4). John probably thought that he was experiencing the greatest joy when he was high, smoking reefer in the backyard, but he came to realize that God could make the joy greater and fuller. He wanted that joy, so he learned how to replace his joy for God's joy.

Can you do that too? Yes. Just get going with these three replacement strategies:

1. *Put yourself in the light.* John surely knew that the things he was "into" were darkness. Either he could live in the darkness by continuing to do all the things that he was doing, or he could start exposing himself to the Light (God).

In 1 John 1 he tells you that you have to start making friends (having fellowship) with the light. That means that you have to start choosing friends who are going to influence you to grow closer to God. (Remember, we talked about that in chapter 3 with Daniel and his friends.)

2. *Enjoy God as your friend.* You see, fellowship doesn't involve just making good friendships with God-honoring friends, it also means that you spend more time letting God be your friend. John says that you need to have fellowship with Jesus. He compares this to going on frequent walks with Him. "If we walk in the light as He Himself is in the light, we have fellowship one with another, and the blood of Jesus His Son cleanses us from all sin" (1 John 1:7, NASB).

Walking with Jesus involves spending time with Him; it involves talking to Him and listening to Him. If you want to stay Christian in high school you need to spend time with Jesus by learning more about Him. You will do this by getting involved in Bible study and reading God's Word.

(Now let's be honest here. The Replacement Principle only replaces what you intend for it to replace. If you think that just going to and sitting in a Bible study will replace your joy, then you're wrong. It will only replace your "party" time with maybe a more "productive" time. The only thing that is replaced is time. But if you want to replace darkness with light then you have to dig in and learn. Read God's Word to learn more about Jesus. Think about what you can do during the day that applies something that you have read from the Bible.)

3. *Talk, and then listen.* This one's about prayer, a great "light" replacement for "darkness." Talk to God about the things you're thinking — then listen. One of the best things you can do to replace darkness with light is to ask God to teach you some things, and then be quiet. God will prompt your heart. Take time, in silence, to hear Him.

The Holy Spirit was sent to you to be the teacher in your life. He prompts you to do things through your conscience, that small voice in your head. He guides you by making the things that you read in the Bible very clear. He leads you by giving you ideas of what you can do to make the stuff you're learning a part of your life. He changes the strong desires to be in darkness to a love for the light.

James and John knew this and they experienced it. They changed from Sons of Thunder to sons of God. They went from loving darkness to walking in light. They transformed from Nitro and Glycerin — anger-filled teenagers — to disciples marked by love. They changed from being the brothers Push and Shove — self-centered, competitive, arrogant boys — to servants. They were revolutionized from Rock and Roll (guys who thought a party lifestyle was fulfilling) to guys who replaced garbage with the fullness of joy.

If you want to stay Christian in high school, let Jesus make you more other-centered, more loving as you learn to walk in light. It really is a great and fulfilling life. Start replacing the garbage with the godly.

Think about it!

---

*If you want to stay a Christian in high school,
you have to be willing to allow Jesus to gradually
replace the rotten stuff with the good stuff.*

THINK IT THROUGH

1. How has Jesus changed you since you first met Him? Can you describe some of the more difficult changes that have taken place?

2. To what extent do you relate to John and James as the Thunder Boys?

3. How often do you feel the need to be better than anyone else at all costs? Is it okay to be first at some things? Explain.

4. What key ideas in this chapter could you take with you into your school tomorrow? How would they make a difference in your attitudes or actions?

5. In what ways would you like to apply the Replacement Principle in your life? What main challenge will you face?

6. In your opinion, what is the most difficult thing about taking on a servant's heart of love? What is the first step to take when overcoming this difficulty?

7. Spend a few minutes in silence, opening your heart to the call of Jesus. What is He saying to you—*right now?*

CHAPTER SIX

TIMOTHY: DEPEND ON JESUS

"Wow, you look like crud! What's wrong?"

"I just can't do this, Paul. I pray every day that God will take this 'thorn' away from me, but He doesn't do it."

"Hey, maybe you aren't trusting God, Tim."

"Oh great! I suck at being Christian, and I don't trust God. This is getting better all the time."

"What do you mean, you don't have a great testimony?" youth pastor Dan asked.

"Well, I grew up in a Christian home," said Lisa. "I always went to church from . . . *birth,* actually. I've never had any bad stuff happen to me, and I've never done any bad stuff to be saved from."

"So what's wrong with that?"

"I hear all these other crazy stories like: 'I was a neo-Nazi, nun-killing drug addict who sacrificed animals to Satan before I was six years old. But then God saved me!' And my story is nothing like that. So, I really don't have a testimony."

"Oh, I get it," Dan said. "You think that people aren't going to be interested in hearing from you because you were never rescued from something spectacular. But did you ever stop to think that the spectacular thing isn't about *what* you were saved from . . . but *that* God saved you?"

Lisa's concern did make sense to Dan. She was traveling to Venezuela with this year's ministry project team, and last week most of the teens had given their testimonies. There hadn't been time for everyone, so Lisa wouldn't be sharing until the next meeting—tomorrow. Over the course of the week, Lisa became more and more concerned about what she could possibly say. Finally, she'd gone to her youth pastor.

"So, are you saying that everybody's testimony is awesome?" Lisa continued.

"Yep. Just put the emphasis on the right thing. The most impressive part of being saved from the consequences of sin is that Jesus did it all. He saved you, and then you're called to depend on Him to keep grow-ing you, day by day, to be more like Him. That whole process is salva-tion, and it's all because of His grace. See? The emphasis is on Jesus—not on your nun-killing past life! What God did was magnifi-cent," Dan said.

"I never thought of it like that, Dan. You're right, my testimony needs to be all about Jesus and how He has been there for me all of my life."

"Right, Lisa. Jesus' blood shed for you is still powerful today in your life. It keeps on saving you from your sin. You don't need to draw atten-tion to the past but to the continuous, present work of salvation."

"Wait, you lost me there," Lisa interrupted. "I know the emphasis needs to be on Jesus, but what do you mean when you say, 'He keeps on saving me' or the 'continuous, present work of salvation'?"

"Lisa, salvation is a process, not a single event. Christ's blood is constantly cleansing you from sin—every day, every hour, every moment. It keeps on saving you from your sin. You're as free from sin as the day you first let Jesus be your Savior."

"But I still have this feeling that 'the Christian thing' is to show people you're perfect. Isn't it a bad witness to nonChristians if they see me mess up?"

///

What would you tell Lisa? Did you grow up in a Christian home too? I did. I've known about Christ all my life, and I trusted Him as my Savior when I was young.

I know that what Jesus did for me was extraordinary, but I didn't like it that my faith was so plain vanilla. I wasn't saved from neo-Nazi animal sacrifice; I was just a little kid! But I too believed I had to be perfect. Those two things made the Christian life relatively uneventful for me . . . and *not* very free.

Lisa is feeling the same way, and it can be a problem. You see, there's a danger in becoming comfortable with faith. It's like falling into a spiritual coma; you just kind of coast on being fake. That's when you stop focusing on what Jesus did—and is *doing* every day—in your life.

Thankfully, a teen in the Bible was a lot like Lisa and me. And maybe a lot like you as well. Let's check out his testimony.

HE GREW UP CHRISTIAN TOO

Meet teenager Timothy. He grew up in a Christian home with his mother, Eunice, and his grandmother, Lois. These faithful women raised and taught Timothy about Jesus from day one. And get this: Timothy's youth pastor was the apostle Paul. Just imagine the conversations between these two. . . .

Timothy comes to youth group one night. He likes to arrive early to hang out with his friends and talk. He's standing there when Paul walks in. "Hey, dude! What's up?" Paul says when he sees Timothy. "How's school going?"

"Okay, I guess," says Timothy. "I hate biology. I don't think the teacher likes me because I talk to my lab partner too much," Timothy replies.

"Well that's easy to fix—just shut up!" Paul says jokingly. Then he grabs Timothy's arm and says, "Let's talk for a couple minutes after the meeting."

Timothy agrees, but starts worrying. *Why does Paul want to talk to me? What did I do? Maybe he wasn't joking when he said that I should stop talking. Maybe he's going to give me a lecture about talking too much in class.*

Soon it was driving him crazy. *I'm going to worry about this all through the meeting!*

Paul got up to give his message. He told the group that God had started a great work in them. "And God will be faithful to finish that work He's started. He has created you for doing good works in the kingdom."

Am I doing any good works? Timothy wondered. *Is that what he wants to talk to me about?* Then he started to think about whether he was doing anything wrong, and then he started to think about whether he was doing anything at all. In a matter of minutes, Timothy went from good, to bad, to boring. *Man, am I confused!*

After youth group, Paul met with Timothy. "Tim, I think God is making you a leader. You can be a great example to your friends. I'd like for you to be a part of our youth ministry leadership team."

"Wow, that would be cool. But I'm not sure I can do that," Timothy replied. "I try to be an example, but then I screw up. Then I try to be perfect, but I feel like I'm being fake. I doubt that God started a good work in me, because nothing spectacular has ever happened to me. I'm just pretty ordinary."

Paul suggested that they meet once a week after school to talk it over. Paul wanted to mentor Timothy to be all that God was making him to be. He knew Timothy could be a great example of faith. And Timothy knew that if he were going to be an example he sure would need some coaching. So Paul became like a spiritual father to Timothy — teaching him, mentoring him, challenging him, and holding him accountable for his spiritual growth. He calls Timothy his spiritual kid in the faith (see 1 Timothy 1:2).

So Paul and Timothy start to meet regularly at Starbucks. "How can I be an example if I'm spiritually *blah?*" Timothy asks. "I can't help my friends that way. And I feel really intimidated talking about God with them, even though I've known God all my life. Anyway, the upper-classmen should be the examples; they're older."

"That's just the point, Timothy. You've known God all your life. You have this spark of faith deep inside of you, in your spirit. You've depended on this spark all your life, and you can fan that spark into a raging fire. God didn't make that spirit in you a spirit of intimidation but one of power and love and discipline."

"How can I do all that, Paul?"

"Well, first understand that God *is* doing a good work in you, so don't let anyone look down on your youth. You don't have to be an upperclassman to be an example. Let your example show in how you rely on Jesus to grow your faith, your love, your purity, your speech, and your conduct. As a matter of fact, Tim, those are the things that are going to fan that spark into a blazing inferno for God." Those Big Five Christian growth areas became their topic of conversation over the many weeks to come.

It's a good topic for any teen, isn't it? Because if you want to stay Christian in high school then you'll have to "fan into flame the gift of God, which is in you" (2 Timothy 1:6). It calls for a complete dependence upon Jesus to grow you in those areas. Then, like Lisa and Timothy, you'll begin to see that being a Christian isn't about being perfect or about how many sins Jesus washed out of your past. It's about Jesus Himself, who saves you, and whom you continually need help from in order to remain faithful.

In fact, being a Christian in high school is more about allowing others to see our shortcomings than trying to demonstrate perfection. As we keep growing, our testimony is about what Jesus is doing to change us. So let's look more closely at some of the things Paul told Timothy about growing big in the Big Five.

FAITH: IT ALL STARTS HERE

The first way Timothy could be an example was in his faith. Faith is believing in something—without full evidence, but with good reason. It's an ongoing, constantly growing thing that's acted out in trust. In other words, it's the place where what you *believe* connects with what you *trust*. Make sense? Timothy had some difficulties with it. . . .

He's had a crummy day at school. He really wants to be an example, and he works hard at it. He prays and asks God to help him do and say the right things so Jesus will be pleased with him. He always asks God to help him make the right decisions. And he constantly asks God to help him control a particular sin habit that keeps tripping him up.

That habit—you know what it is for you. Paul had a code name for it; he called it his "thorn in his flesh." It's so annoying because we can usually function with it, but the constant battle wears us down. On the other hand, sometimes it makes life so painful that we stop functioning at all. That's how Paul saw the sinful habit in his life. It was an annoying little thing that made life hugely miserable at times.

So Timothy, still smarting from his rotten day, stops by the church to talk with Paul. Plopping down on the couch across from Paul's desk, Timothy pulls some Skittles out of his book bag and starts popping them.

"Wow, you look like crud!" Paul says. "What's wrong?"

"I just can't do this, Paul. I mean, it's so hard to be a Christian in high school. I pray every day that God will take this . . . 'thorn' . . . away from me, but He doesn't do it. I really suck at being a Christian."

"Hey, maybe you aren't trusting God, Tim," Paul replies.

"Oh great! I suck at being Christian, *and* I don't trust God. This is getting better all the time," Timothy says sarcastically as he tosses about four Skittles into his mouth.

"Chill out, Tim. That's not what I mean. Just listen for a minute."

Paul explains to Timothy that Satan has two strategies for making Christians live defeated lives. The *first* one is that he tempts you. You can probably relate to this one. I can! The things that we *don't* want to do, he makes those things strong desires within us. Paul talks about this all through the book of Romans when he refers to the fact that we have this sinful nature in us that makes us very vulnerable to Satan's temptations. (Take a moment right now to see Paul's real-life struggle with temptation. Read Romans 7:15-24. Recognize anyone you know?)

Paul compares this struggle to a war between the Good Me and the Evil Me. The Good Me knows and wants what is right and honoring to God. The Evil Me doesn't give a rip and just wants to satisfy self-centered desires.

Satan starts to talk to the sinful nature (or the Evil Me). He appeals to those desires that don't honor God. His persuasions are strong and often make sense to you. You start to think things like, "This isn't going to hurt anyone" or "I can do this just one more time" or "Every teenager does this." The next thing you know —*badaboom*, you act on the temptation. You've gone from *being tempted* (nothing wrong with that) to *acting it out* (now it's sin). Satan wants you to sin, so he goes all out with the temptation.

After you fall, Satan kicks the process into *second* gear. This strategy involves accusing you. He starts talking to the Good Me, the part that wants to please God. He tells you that you're pond scum —you blew it, you worthless loser! "You can never be the person that God wants you to be. You will always fail."

Have you heard that voice before? Satan tells you that God doesn't love you, that your sin is the worst event in human history. In fact, he will tell you anything to keep you defeated. Once he has you down from the temptation, he needs to keep you down with defeat and guilt. The voice of accusation works wonders.

"But that's where faith comes in, Tim-bo!" says a smiling apostle Paul. "God said that He started a good work in you and that He would be faithful to complete it (see Philippians 1:6). You have to trust that God is making you the person that He wants you to be. So look at that thorn as an opportunity to run into God's arms and give Him control over that habit. He never will get tired of you, because He keeps loving you, no matter what you do. Faith means trusting in God's love, grace, mercy, and His salvation that keeps on saving you. That means when you fall to temptation, get up! Run to God, and give Him control."

"But it's hard, Paul, not to feel so guilty when I fail!"

"Hey, there's no condemnation to those who are in Christ, Tim. So which part of *no condemnation* don't you get? Trust what God says He's doing *in* you and *through* you."

Paul told Timothy the same thing he told the believers in Romans 4:25–5:4 (MSG).

> *The sacrificed Jesus made us fit for God, set us right with God. By entering through faith into what God has always wanted to do for us — set us right with him, make us fit for him — we have it all together with God because of our Master Jesus. And that's not all: We throw open our doors to God and discover at the same moment that he has already thrown open his door to us. We find ourselves standing where we always hoped we might stand — out in the wide open spaces of God's grace and glory, standing tall and shouting our praise.*
>
> *There's more to come: We continue to shout our praise even when we're hemmed in with troubles, because we know how troubles can develop passionate patience in us, and how that*

patience in turn forges the tempered steel of virtue, keeping us
alert for whatever God will do next.

Here's the point for every high schooler: You're perfectly accepted by God because you trusted Jesus for your salvation. Not only that, but you have a direct connection to God—a huge, open door to Him— because of faith. That faith gives you peace, even in troubled times. The peace comes because what Jesus *did* and *does* for you, not because of what you do. Jesus gives you the access to God; Jesus becomes the anchor that makes you stable.

WHAT'S LOVE GOT TO DO WITH IT?

One evening Paul told the youth group that every believer was given a spiritual gift or gifts to build up the church. So Timothy wanted to know what the best gifts were—so he could get them. "Whoa, slow down, son," Paul said. "You're missing a very important point about the most important thing." Paul explained that love is the greatest thing, not the spiritual gifts. "Concentrate on being a lover, Tim. People see God working in us and through us when we are compassionate and loving, not because we claim certain skills." It was the same thing Paul told the Corinthian believers—

> *If I speak in the tongues of men and of angels, but have not love,*
> *I am only a resounding gong or a clanging cymbal. If I have*
> *the gift of prophecy and can fathom all mysteries and all knowl-*
> *edge, and if I have a faith that can move mountains, but have*
> *not love, I am nothing. If I give all I possess to the poor and sur-*
> *render my body to the flames, but have not love, I gain nothing.*
> *Love is patient, love is kind. It does not envy, it does not*
> *boast, it is not proud. It is not rude, it is not self-seeking, it is*

not easily angered, it keeps no record of wrongs. Love does not
delight in evil but rejoices with the truth. It always protects,
always trusts, always hopes, always perseveres.
Love never fails. (1 Corinthians 13:1-8)

As you can see, this love thing is a *big deal*. You've already seen it in James' and John's lives. Love is the defining mark of a Christian. Jesus said that people will know that you are Christian by the way you love. As a Christian you have the opportunity to let people see Jesus. Your friends and family will see Jesus when He loves through you. You get to be a pipeline that His love flows through. If you want to stay Christian in high school, then ask God to help you to love others. If you pray that prayer to Him, you might find your heart breaking more over things that you never dreamed would touch you.

I issued that prayer-challenge to my college students. I also told them to watch out, because if they prayed that prayer then God would, in fact, honor it. They would start to become more loving. Then I invited them to ask God to make them more loving toward "difficult" people. To ask God to help them see life situations through loving eyes. To pray that God would help them just listen-in-love whenever their friends poured out their problems.

Two weeks later, one of the guys asked if he could meet with me. He was a big football player, and the first thing he said when he walked into my office was: "You messed me up!"

I didn't know what I'd done to mess him up, so I was very concerned. "I've been praying that God would make me more loving," he said. "And it's *working!*"

His heart was breaking for people. He'd cry when his friends talked about their struggles. He constantly thought about the welfare of those around him.

"What's happening to me, Doc? Am I going crazy?"

"Maybe you're going deeper into the heart and will of Jesus," I suggested. "But do you want to stop?"

He told me, in no uncertain terms, that he did *not* want to stop. Because he was seeing Jesus work through him. It was the most awesome thing that had ever happened to him. In the days that followed I watched this guy in action. His friends started to want what he had. He had become an example of being a loving Christian.

PURITY: MORE THAN A SEX THING

Timothy really wanted to know what God's will was for his life. He decided that he and Paul should talk about this one. "Maybe you already know what that will is, Timothy," Paul said.

"*What?* But I have no idea what I'm supposed to be doing in the years ahead!"

"No, Tim. That will all come to you as you move forward with the Lord. Because God's will is what He wants for you *right now*. It's a daily thing, developing a passion and the number-one life priority of pleasing God, guided by His Spirit within you. And since that's true, you can know His will for you. It's to make it your heart's desire to be pure, step-by-step, throughout your day."

"That's it? Just be pure, step-by-step, as I'm guided by the Spirit?" It almost sounded too easy! Timothy could do this if he were to run way from lust and run after faith, love, and peace.

"Just walk in the Lord, Tim. That's the purity I'm talking about," said Paul.

Another word for the process is the Bible term *sanctification*. Paul told Timothy that his life purpose was to be pleasing to the Lord. God's will was that His children be sanctified and live in purity. The best way for a high school student to do this is to decide to stay sexually pure. Timothy knew that if he was going to stay Christian in high school, he needed to let Jesus keep him pure in every way, but especially sexually pure.

Can you make the same decision? God's will for you is your purity. In chapter 4 we saw how Joseph did it—he ran when temptation hit. When Paul talked to Timothy about sanctification, he used an example of sexual purity. But it also means that you operate out of a pure mind and a pure heart. That means your motives are pure, conversations are pure, desires are pure, wants and needs are pure—all that you do is pure. And as you do this, the Holy Spirit will be your helper.

(How about taking a breather at this point in the chapter? Open your Bible and read 1 Thessalonians 4:1-12, where Paul explains this more fully. Then ask Jesus to help you be pure. That's God's will, and that's one way you can stay Christian in high school.)

SPEECH: WATCH YOUR MOUTH!

Timothy was a normal teenager, and sometimes his language with his friends was different than it was at home or church. One day Timothy was talking with his friends about another friend. They were concerned this other friend was getting into some questionable things. Somewhere in the conversation, he and his friends began talking about "what they heard." What started as *concern* suddenly changed to *gossip*. Making matters worse, the gossip started to include some off-color joking, and that broke the ice for a few swear words thrown in for good measure.

This conversation was in full swing when Paul walked by. The result? A new topic of conversation for Timothy's next mentoring meeting: how you *shouldn't* talk, and how you *should* talk.

1. *It* **shouldn't** *be like this!* Let's listen in. "I just finished writing a letter to the Christians in Ephesus, Tim," says Paul as he booted up his laptop so that he could read the draft of the letter to Timothy. "Here's what I'm telling them: 'Do not let any unwholesome talk come out of your mouths, but only what is helpful for building others up according to their needs, that it may benefit those who listen.'" (Ephesians 4:29).

Paul told Timothy that the Ephesians needed to learn to control the way they talked. Some people thought it was okay to sort of lie, twist the truth a little, or not tell the entire truth. Others were talking about people behind their backs. And others said whatever they wanted in bursts of rage. Their language needed to be wholesome and decent. "Nor should there be obscenity, foolish talk or coarse joking, which are out of place, but rather thanksgiving" (Ephesians 5:4).

Timothy knew right away that he probably should have changed the subject or guided the conversation more away from gossiping when he and the guys were talking about their friend. He probably realized that the off-color jokes, the swearing, the lewd comments were all very inappropriate for Christians. Timothy knew that it was hard to stay Christian in high school. He heard this kind of talk all day long, and he knew not to talk like that at school but sometimes he dropped his guard with his Christian friends.

2. *Here's how it* **should** *be.* Paul opened another file on his laptop and continued: "Here's what I'm writing to the Colossians: 'Let your conversation be always full of grace, seasoned with salt, so that you may know how to answer everyone' (Colossians 4:6).

"Salt does three things, Timothy. It brings out the good flavor of something, it makes you thirsty, and it acts as a preservative. So, if a conversation starts to turn bad, you can redirect it by talking about good things and being gracious. And if your talk is good and encouraging, then most people will *thirst* for more of it."

"But how is my speech like a preservative?" Timothy asked.

"Well, when you talk, you naturally bring the Holy Spirit into the conversation because the Spirit lives within you. The Spirit's job is to preserve the world from sin. He dwells in believers so we can bring the goodness and light of God into a dark world. One of the ways that He does this is by guiding our speech. So our speech preserves the world from evil, just like salt preserves foods."

If you are still thinking, then you are realizing that the same things that applied for Timothy apply for you too. Remember that what comes out of your mouth reflects what's in your heart. Therefore, the only way to keep control of your speech is to let the Holy Spirit have control over your entire life.

In the final part of his letter to the Colossians, Paul wrote that they should be controlled by the Holy Spirit, just like a drunk person is controlled by liquor! Timothy liked that illustration. He began asking the Holy Spirit to control his speech more. Not a bad action to follow!

CONDUCT: DO BEHAVE YOURSELF

Timothy spent so much time around Paul that he could imitate many of Paul's idiosyncrasies and mannerisms. Needless to say, Timothy's youth group got a big kick out of Tim's impressions of Paul. One thing that Timothy picked up on was a phrase that Paul often said over and over when he taught: "Conduct yourself in a manner worthy of the gospel of Jesus!" Timothy could say it just like Paul did. And every time Tim repeated it, he became more aware that he needed to practice it.

Timothy had to work at that in the most routine situations, every single day. One evening he's sitting in front of his computer IM-ing his friends. His mom calls: "Take out the garbage, Timothy!"

"Okay, in a minute."

"Now, Timothy. I need you to do this immediately." But Timothy just ignores her. After all, how insensitive can she be? He obviously needs to meet his friends' needs. He keeps his online conversation going.

After a few minutes he hears, "Timothy, if you don't get that garbage out right now, you'll be grounded from that computer until you go to college." Timothy gets up and walks into the kitchen, muttering a few choice things under his breath, leaving a trail of attitude all the way through the house. He stands in front of the garbage bag and starts to pull it out of the basket. As he does, some grapefruit rinds and old coffee grounds splatter on the floor. He leaves the mess sitting there.

"Pick it up," his mom says as she stands over him, watching every move.

Timothy gives more attitude, and his mom confronts that attitude. She tells him he'd better change it or he will pay the price. Now Timothy feels like he's being attacked and misunderstood, so he tries to explain, raising his voice. Mom becomes more annoyed by this, and cautions Timothy about his tone. Timothy gets more upset with that, because he doesn't think she's listening. So he pulls out the old "Yeah, whatever" line. Now Mom feels totally disrespected, so she says, "You need to watch your conduct, young man, because this is not the way Jesus would want one of His followers to act."

Ouch! Been there?

Timothy now recalls Paul's favorite line: "Conduct yourself in a manner worthy of the gospel of Jesus." He knows something needs to change.

Paul once told his youth group that their conduct should be "others-centered." That meant that they were supposed to work hard at seeing other people as more important than themselves. He challenged them to not just look out for their own personal interests but also for the interests of others. Paul knew that if their conduct was going to be like Jesus, then *their attitudes had to be like Jesus' too.* So he reminded them that Jesus had an "others-centered" attitude. Jesus was so others-centered that He reduced Himself by taking on flesh and dying on a cross for others.

When Paul and Timothy talked, Timothy was reminded that conduct wasn't just about behavior; it was all about attitude *and* behavior. If Timothy wanted his behavior to change, then he had to change his attitude. Jesus had to be in control of his head, heart, and hands. If there was no heart change, then the behavior would never change.

But how, exactly, does a heart begin to change? If we think in terms of computers, we could say we've got to program our hearts with the right things. Paul once wrote: "Brothers, whatever is true, whatever is noble, whatever is right, whatever is pure, whatever is lovely, whatever is admirable—if anything is excellent or praiseworthy—think about such things" (Philippians 4:8).

The things that you think about and the stuff that you listen to affect your attitude. I have found that when you try to eliminate things from your life, it becomes easy to get defeated. You'll have an easier time if you use the Replacement Principle we talked about in the chapter on James and John. In case you forgot, the Replacement Principle is putting something good or positive into your life so that it pushes out or replaces the thing that is negative. For example, if you say that you're no longer going to listen to your friends talk trash about their parents, and think that's cool, good for you. But it only focuses on what you *won't* do. Now, add something positive that you *will* do. One idea may be to think about ways to honor your parents. Replacement—get it!

That's the point that Paul was driving at in Philippians 4:8 when he talked about "thinking on such things." You might find out that thinking Christian leads to an attitude that's Christian and makes you behave Christian. God is all about transforming you. He started a good work in you—remember.

Timothy knew the pressures of trying to stay Christian in high school. He knew what it was like to feel inadequate and then think that he had to be perfect. He wanted to be an example to others, but he didn't know what that actually meant. It seemed like an overwhelming task, until he dug into Paul's teachings. Letting go of perfection while depending on Jesus to grow him—that was the key.

Is Timothy really so different from you? He was a real teenager with struggles. The advice Paul gave Timothy is the same advice that he gives you.

The great thing is that Timothy ended up being a fine pastor-leader in one of the early churches. He followed Paul's advice about being an example and depending on Jesus. Timothy stayed Christian through high school, and God kept opening doors of service to him. God's plan is the same for you.

Think about it!

*If you want to stay a Christian in high school,
don't be perfect, just be dependent (on Jesus).*

THINK IT THROUGH

1. Go back to Lisa's struggle at the beginning of this chapter. Have you ever felt as she did about having a "great testimony"?

2. In your opinion, what is the difference between trying to be perfect and pursuing excellence through depending on Christ?

3. Do you agree that our Christian witness is more about allowing others to see our shortcomings? What happens in your relationships when you reveal your flaws?

4. What is your definition of the word *sanctification?* How do you see this process at work in your own life?

5. What is your particular "thorn in the flesh"? How do the teachings in Romans 7 and 8 speak to you about it?

6. How realistic is it to think that a teen could grow strong in the Big Five? What is your experience with them?

7. What does "depending on Jesus" mean to you? Think: When has He most powerfully met your need? How could that past experience help give you hope for the future?

POP QUIZ

Why is th1nkbooks.com spelled with a "1" instead
of an "i"?
   a) it holds deep symbolic meaning
   b) www.thinkbooks.com was already taken
   c) the owl told us to do it

Check out upcoming releases from TH1NK books,
sign up for our street teams, and chat with other
readers. Bookmark www.th1nkbooks.com.

1-800-366-7788
www.th1nkbooks.com